# Thomas Alva Edison

## Bringer of Light

by Carol Greene

CHILDRENS PRESS ™

CHICAGO

## PICTURE ACKNOWLEDGMENTS

From the Collections of Henry Ford Museum and Greenfield
Village—Frontispiece, page 8, 66 (top), 67 (bottom), 68 (bottom)
U.S. Department of the Interior, National Park Service, Edison
National Historic Site—pages 14, 20, 28, 67 (top), 73, 112, 120
Courtesy of The Henry Ford Museum, Dearborn, Michigan—page
66 (bottom)
Historical Pictures Services, Chicago—pages 68 (top), 71 (top), 94
The Granger Collection—pages 69, 70, 71 (bottom), 72
Cover illustration by Len W. Meents

Library of Congress Cataloging in Publication Data

Greene, Carol
    Thomas Alva Edison, bringer of light.

    Includes index.
    Summary: A biography of the ingenious American whose
inventions include the electric light bulb, the phonograph,
and other useful items.
    1. Edison, Thomas A. (Thomas Alva), 1847-1931—
Biography—Juvenile literature. [1. Edison, Thomas A.
(Thomas Alva), 1847-1931. 2. Inventors] I. Title. II. Series.
TK140.E3G73    1985      621.3′092′4 [B] [92]      84-23247
ISBN 0-516-03213-5

    2 3 4 5 6 7 8 9 10 R 94 93 92 91 90 89 88 87 86

# Table of Contents

A photograph of Thomas Edison taken in 1851 when he was four years old.

## Chapter 1

# THE WONDERING BOY

To say that Thomas Alva Edison was curious would be like saying the ocean is damp. He wondered about *every-thing*—how, why, when, where, who, and what if.

Before he was even two, his big sister Marion's boyfriend gave him a silver coin. It was a bribe to leave the boyfriend and Marion alone for a while.

Little Al (that's what he was called then) was too young to wonder what the coin would buy. He loved it because it was so beautiful. Look at how it spun around! *How* did it do that?

And *why* did hens and geese sit on their eggs? He wasn't much older when he wondered that.

To keep them warm and hatch them, his mother, Nancy Edison, told him.

And if a hen or goose could do it, why couldn't he?

Several hours later, his family found him in a neighbor's barn. He was perched on a nest that had been full of eggs. Now most of the eggs were on the seat of young Al's pants.

But the experiment wasn't a total failure. He had learned something. Little boys can't hatch eggs.

Nancy Elliott Edison had not had an easy life. She had taught school in upper Canada when she was just a young girl. Then, at seventeen, she had married Samuel Edison, Jr.

Sam was a strong, handsome man. But he was also hotheaded, restless, and not too practical. He and Nancy had four children while they lived in Vienna, Ontario. Then Sam got mixed up in a plot against the Canadian government.

He was off marching in the woods when he learned that government soldiers were after him. Sam dashed back to Vienna to say good-bye to Nancy and the children. Then he stretched his long legs and ran for the United States border, eighty miles away. He made it.

While Nancy waited with the children in Canada, Sam drifted down to Milan, Ohio. Milan was going to be a big city someday. Everyone said so. Folks there were building the Huron Canal to connect the town to other waterways. One day they would be able to ship goods right on through to the Atlantic Ocean. Yes, Milan would end up an important port.

Now, ports need warehouses, thought Sam Edison. And warehouses need roofs and roofs need shingles. So why not start a shingle mill?

With some help from a friend, Alva Bradley, that was exactly what Sam did. Then he decided it was time to send for Nancy and the children. And before long, two more children were born.

Nancy Edison's troubles weren't over, though. The children did not seem to do well in Milan. Before long, Carlisle, one of their boys, died at the age of six. The next year three-year-old Samuel died. In 1847 little Eliza also died at the age of three.

But 1847 brought a birth, too. Snow had fallen all through the night. Then, in the early morning hours of February 11, a puny little boy was born. Sam and Nancy called him Thomas after one of Sam's brothers. They chose Alva as a middle name in honor of the friend who had helped with the shingle mill.

So there he was—Thomas Alva Edison. He had fair hair and blue eyes. His head was so large that the doctor thought he might have brain fever. (He didn't.)

From that day on, Nancy Edison's life didn't become easier. But it certainly became more interesting.

When Al was about three years old he began to wonder what went on in the huge grain elevators down by the canal. He climbed to the top of one and peered over the edge. Someone was unloading grain at the time. How it whirled and swirled! Al leaned over for a better look.

Then he lost his balance. Down he fell into the dusty, choking grain. Fortunately someone spotted him and fished him out before he drowned in grain.

Not all of his adventures had such happy endings, though. Years later he wrote about one of the sad ones:

When I was a small boy at Milan, and about
five years old, I and the son of the proprietor of

the largest store in the town, whose age was about the same as mine, went down in a gully in the outskirts of the town to swim in a small creek. After playing in the water a while, the boy with me disappeared in the creek. I waited around for him to come up but as it was getting dark I concluded to wait no longer and went home. Some time in the night I was awakened and asked about the boy. It seems the whole town was out with lanterns and had heard that I was last seen with him. I told them how I had waited and waited, etc. They went to the creek and pulled out his body.

About a year after that, when he was six, Al decided to light a bonfire. It was a windy fall day and he couldn't get the leaves to stay in neat piles. So he took them inside a barn and started his bonfire there.

A moment later the whole barn was in flames. Al ran out, unharmed. But the barn burned to the ground and, if the wind had been much stronger, the whole town might have caught fire.

Nancy Edison was pleased with her son for admitting he had started the fire. But Sam Edison looked grim. He had punished Al again and again for his irresponsible pranks. Nothing seemed to stop the naughtiness. Well, this time he would teach young Al a lesson he would never forget.

A few days after the fire, he marched the boy to the village square. There, in front of a small crowd of people, he gave him a public whipping.

Sam was right. Al never forgot that whipping. But he didn't stop wondering, either.

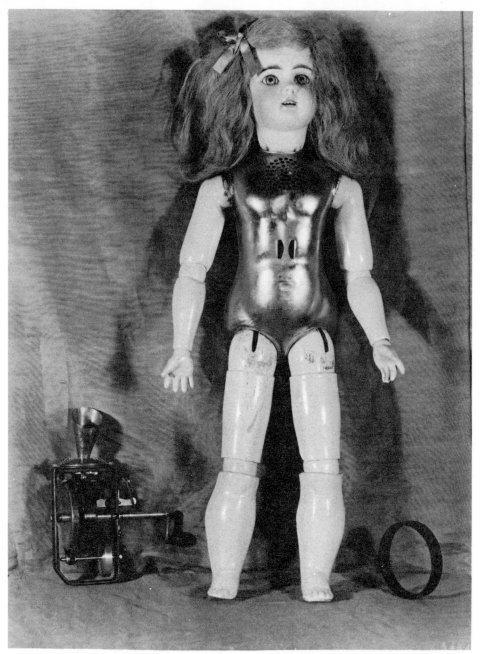

Edison made a talking doll in the late 1880s.

# Chapter 2

# SCHOOL DAYS—MORE OR LESS

The people of Milan made a mistake—a big one. When railroad builders wanted to bring track through, the town turned them down. What did Milan need with a railroad? It had a canal, didn't it?

So the railroad bypassed Milan. Soon businesses discovered that shipping by rail was cheaper and faster than shipping by water. They began to build factories and warehouses near railroads. And the people of Milan were left high and dry—in spite of their canal.

So much for the shingle mill, thought Sam Edison. Time to move on. He and Nancy and the children packed up their belongings and headed north to the town of Port Huron, Michigan.

They ended up in a big old house at Fort Gratiot, a United States Army base just north of the town. There seven-year-old Al came down with a serious case of scarlet fever. While Nancy nursed him, Sam worked at setting himself up in business. He had a job looking after the fort's lighthouse and tending the boiler that made the foghorn blow. But he was thinking about the lumber, grain, and feed businesses, too. Might as well try several things in case one went bad.

At that time children started school fairly late. Al's poor health delayed his start even more. But finally, when he was eight, his parents enrolled him in a one-room school run by the Reverend and Mrs. G.B. Engle.

The Reverend Mr. Engle was not a gentle man. He believed that applying his cane to students helped them learn faster. His wife, some said, was even more harsh. Al hated school.

Doctors are now beginning to understand that unhappiness can cause people to become sick more easily. Maybe it was Al's experiences at school that gave him so many physical problems that year. In any case, he had never been very strong and that winter he caught cold after cold. Most of them settled in his ears, which filled with fluid. Then he couldn't hear very well and that got him into trouble with his teachers.

One day he overheard the Reverend Mr. Engle tell someone that Al's mind was "addled." For Al it was the last straw. He thundered out of the school, ran all the way home, and told his mother what he had heard.

The next day Nancy had a talk with Engle. Her son's mind was most certainly *not* addled.

Then why wasn't he learning anything? demanded the schoolmaster.

The argument went on and on. By the time it was over, Nancy's mind was made up. Her boy wasn't going to *that* school anymore. Why, she could teach him better at home!

What happened next is not too clear. Probably Nancy did teach Al at home part of the time. But he also went to another private school—which he liked.

When he was eleven, he went to a public school in Port Huron. It was at that school that he pulled another of his famous pranks.

What if, he and a girl in his class wondered—what if they baited a fishing hook and let it down from a second-story window?

They did it—and caught a chicken that squawked and flapped all the way up.

Al also caught another whipping.

By then he had most likely put the Reverend G.B. Engle out of his mind. But Engle never forgot him. Thirty years later, when Edison was a famous man, he received a letter from his former teacher. Engle was seventy-six and not too well off. He just wanted to point out to Mr. Edison that his father had never paid the twenty-five dollars due for Edison's schooling. Since Edison had plenty of money now, could he send a little aid?

Those grim months in Engle's little school must have flashed through the grown Edison's mind again. (He had once described them to someone as "repulsive.") But by now he could afford a little forgiveness as well as some aid. So he sent a check for twenty-five dollars.

One thing Nancy Edison did teach her son was to love books. Two of the books she gave him were R.G. Parker's *School of Natural Philosophy* and an old *Dictionary of Science*. From them he learned how to set up and work experiments—real *scientific* experiments. Soon his room was full of chemicals, wire, and bits of metal.

Years later he told a newspaper reporter, "My mother was the making of me."

But he added at another time, "My mother's ideas and mine differed at times, especially when I got experimenting and mussed up things."

It's not hard to understand Nancy's point of view. Not many mothers would be overjoyed to find sulfuric acid eating into their furniture and floor.

To the basement! she ordered. Al went.

By this time his sisters Marion and Harriet Ann had married. His brother Pitt, a grown man, was the only other one left at home. But for some reason Al worried about other people getting into his beloved chemicals in the basement. So he calmly—and dishonestly—labeled them all "Poison."

Chemical experiments weren't the only kind that interested him. Like many boys at that time, he was fascinated by the telegraph, invented not long before by Samuel F.B. Morse.

Of course Al had to build his own telegraph set. Then he spent hours working to improve it and practicing Morse code. Whenever his family needed him, they knew just where to find him—in the basement.

Sam Edison wasn't very happy about all this. He thought his son should be more like other boys. Why couldn't Al work outside, play sports, and read real literature instead of those science manuals? Was he stupid or something?

For a while Al did work outside. He and a hired boy, Michael Oates, tried their hands at raising vegetables and selling them around town. They earned a good bit of money that way, too.

But before long Al tired of the project. First of all, it was very hard work. But, even more important, it kept him away from his experiments.

Sam even tried to change the boy's reading habits. He gave him a penny for each book of serious literature he read.

So, along with other books, Al read Thomas Paine's *The Age of Reason*. He loved it. But he used the pennies he earned to buy more chemicals.

Then, in 1859 when Al was twelve, the railroad came to Port Huron. It was a great event for everyone in town. But it was an especially great event for young Al Edison, because the railroad brought him his first real job.

When Edison was a teenager he was a newsboy on the Grand Trunk Railroad.

## Chapter 3

# THE CANDY BUTCHER

The railroad, it seemed, needed a newsboy. He would get on the train at Port Huron at seven-fifteen each morning. There he would sell newspapers and refreshments to the travelers. Some four hours later the train would pull into Detroit. During a five-hour layover, the boy could read, stroll around, take a nap, or do whatever he liked. Late in the afternoon he'd return to Port Huron, again peddling his wares. The train would get in around eight or nine in the evening.

Railroad newsboys were called "candy butchers." They weren't paid a regular salary. Instead they earned a little money for each item they sold. Al wanted the job badly.

His mother didn't like the idea one bit. After all, her son was only twelve—and small for his age. But Sam Edison felt differently. He wasn't doing well in his various businesses. Al wasn't doing well in school because of his poor hearing. It would be best for all, Sam decided, if the boy got a job.

He wouldn't stop reading books, promised Al. Look at all the time he would have during that long layover in Detroit! And he would have more money to buy what he needed for his scientific experiments, too.

So finally Nancy gave in. Early one morning she went with her son to the Port Huron station. Maybe she felt a little better about the whole thing when the conductor, Alex Stephenson, promised to keep an eye on Al.

It wasn't too unusual in those days for children to go to work at an early age. Some—like Al Edison—were glad to do it. He later called his years with the railroad "the happiest time of my life. I was just old enough to have a good time in the world," he added in a newspaper interview, "but not old enough to understand any of its troubles."

While he was having that good time, Al was also learning— especially during the layovers in Detroit. There he could wander along the waterfront and meet people from all over the world. Or he could stay in the railroad yard and watch the men switch cars, repair equipment, and telegraph to other stations. Eventually he joined the Detroit Public Library. (It cost two dollars for a card back then.)

"I didn't read a few books," he wrote years later. "I read the library."

It happened that the baggage car where Al spent most of his time had a lot of free space. It also just so happened that chemicals were one of Detroit's chief products.

Al quickly put those two facts together and had a long talk with Alex Stephenson. Before long he had set up a portable laboratory. It was probably the first one ever on a train.

In fact, the only part of Al's job that he didn't like was the drive home from the Port Huron station after dark. The road took him past a cemetery where three hundred soldiers were buried. They had died during a cholera epidemic in 1832.

But might not a few of them still march around at night in ghostly form? That's what bothered Al. Sometimes when he got to the cemetery, he just closed his eyes and let the horse have its way. If there were any marching going on, he wasn't going to see it.

One night the head of a shipping company in Port Huron asked Al to run an important errand. The captain of one of his ships had died. Would Al walk fourteen miles through the forest to the home of a retired captain? He would have to get there in time for the captain to catch the morning train. He'd be paid fifteen dollars for the errand.

"Make it twenty-five dollars," said Al. He didn't want to go alone. He would use the extra ten to hire another boy to go with him. The shipping head agreed.

So Al and his friend set off along the dark forest trail, each carrying a lantern. It was raining. Soon the boys began to hear noises. Bears! they thought. There really were bears in that forest. The problem with bears was that you couldn't even climb a tree to get away from them. When you got up a tree, you might find one waiting for you!

Suddenly one of the lanterns went out. The two boys drew closer to the light of the remaining one. Then it went out, too.

There was only one thing left to do. The boys sagged against a tree and cried. Then they stumbled on in the dark.

Finally, just as dawn broke, they reached the captain's house.

"In my whole life," wrote Al years later, "I never spent such a night of horror."

But most of his job was fun and he thoroughly enjoyed it. The Civil War was being fought at that time and people were eager for news of the battles.

On April 6, 1862, Union and Confederate armies fought a tremendous battle at Shiloh. Al heard about it in Detroit. Usually he sold only about a hundred newspapers on the return run to Port Huron. But this battle was *news*. If people only realized that, they would buy a lot more papers.

Al had an idea. He shoved his way into the offices of the *Detroit Free Press*. He had enough money for only three hundred papers. But he talked the editor into letting him have seven hundred more on credit. Then he paid a visit to the railroad's telegraph operator in Detroit. Would the man please send news of the battle to each station along the line? Al would give him refreshments, newspapers, and magazine subscriptions in return.

The telegraph operator agreed and sent off his messages. Telegraph operators at the stations chalked up the news on bulletin boards. In a magazine article many years later, Al told what happened next:

When I got to the first station on the run . . . the platform was crowded with men and women. After one look at the crowd I raised the price to ten cents. I sold thirty-five papers. At Mount Clemens, where I usually sold six papers, the crowd was there too. . . . I raised the price from ten cents to fifteen. . . . It had been my practice at Port Huron to jump from the train about one quarter of a mile from the station where the train generally slackened speed. I had drawn several loads of sand to this point and had become quite expert. The little Dutch boy with the horse usually met me there. When the wagon approached the outskirts of town I was met by a large crowd. I then yelled: "Twenty-five cents, gentlemen—I haven't enough to go around!"

His plan was a huge success and Al learned something important.

"It was then," he said later, "it struck me that the telegraph was just about the best thing going, for it was the notices on the bulletin board that had done the trick. I determined at once to become a telegrapher."

But there was another reason why Al wanted to become a telegrapher. His hearing was growing worse and worse.

Sometimes people's voices swirled around him unheard. But he could always hear the clack-clack of the telegraph. So he began practicing on little sets he built himself.

For a while people believed that Al lost his hearing when the conductor, Alex Stephenson, boxed him on the ears. It is true that Al got into big trouble with Mr. Stephenson one time. Some of his chemicals fell to the floor and started a fire in the baggage car. Stephenson managed to put it out and then informed his candy butcher chemicals had to go.

But the only physical contact anyone had with Al's ears happened when a trainman saved the boy's life. Al was late getting to the train one morning. It was already moving when he leaped for a freight car, his arms full of newspapers. He just made the last step and would have fallen under the train if a man hadn't grabbed him by the ears and pulled him on board.

That, said doctors later, might have damaged the ligaments that attach the ears to the head. But it would have had nothing to do with Al's deafness. The deafness most likely came from all those early ear infections. They had never been properly treated. In time they probably had damaged Al's middle ear—permanently.

Meanwhile, Al had to go on working. Sam Edison wasn't doing any better with his businesses. Al kept trying to come up with new ways to make money. One day he had an idea. Why not put out his own newspaper?

With money saved from that day of the Battle of Shiloh, he bought a little printing press and some type. Then he set up shop in the baggage car. Soon the *Grand Trunk Herald* was rolling off the press.

Al's news was mostly local tidbits, gossip, and information about the railroad. His spelling was atrocious. But he had a lively style—and people do like to read about themselves. Soon he was selling four hundred copies of the paper at three cents a copy.

Then another boy, who worked for a printer in Port Huron, talked Al into becoming partners. They called their paper *Paul Pry*. It included some spicy gossip. Legend says that one man got so angry at Al that he threw him into the Saint Clair River. (But he probably only *threatened* to do it.)

Then one day Al was standing on the station platform in Mount Clemens. A heavy boxcar was being shifted out of a siding. As Al waited, he watched the men work. Suddenly he saw a three-year-old boy, son of the stationmaster, playing on the track. The boxcar was headed straight for him.

Al threw down his papers, ran for the little boy, grabbed him, and hauled him to safety. Later he tried to tell people that what he had done was nothing. He had never been in any real danger.

But James Mackenzie, the stationmaster, disagreed. He offered to reward Al by teaching him to operate the telegraph. At last Al's dream seemed about to come true.

Edison poses with his tin foil phonograph in his lab at Menlo Park.

Chapter 4

# THE WANDERING BOY

For five months Al worked with Mackenzie. He practiced
sending and receiving messages at Mount Clemens. He also
practiced at home. To do this, he strung wire from a cave in
the Edison backyard to the home of a friend, Jim Clancy, a
mile away. Then, using homemade sets, the boys telegraphed
newspaper stories to each other.

To become a first-class telegrapher took a lot of time and
talent. Al couldn't hope to be first-class in five short months.
But he felt proud when he sent his first long word—
*Mississippi*. And eventually he grew fast enough to be a
"plug"—a second-class telegrapher.

In the summer of 1863, at age sixteen, Al began working
part-time in the Port Huron telegraph office. It took up one
corner of the town jewelry store. Not many messages went
in or out of Port Huron, so Al didn't have much to do. He
didn't get paid much either—twenty-five dollars a month.
But at least he had time to go on with his experiments.

One day he and a couple of friends decided to mix various
substances with battery acid. Suddenly the people of Port
Huron heard a terrific boom. Out of the jewelry store
stumbled Al and his friends. Al was also out of a job.

He took off for a military base near Washington, D.C. The Civil War was still going on and the Union army needed telegraphers. They took one look at young Al, though, and decided that they didn't need him.

Back home he went and once again James Mackenzie stepped in to help. This time he found a job for Al as telegrapher for the railroad at Stratford, Ontario. But Al lost that job too, although he said later that it wasn't his fault. Someone had sent a message too late and two trains almost had collided.

Still, the railroad officials blamed the mix-up on Al and were ready to throw him in prison. Fortunately he managed to sneak away and escape across the border into the United States.

In the early days of the telegraph, telegraphers were often wanderers. A young man might take off for a city across the country with only a few cents in his pocket. He could always find jobs along the way. And if he felt like going on to someplace else a few months later—well, that was all right, too.

Al soon slipped into this wandering life. For some reason he just couldn't settle down. Every time he tried, something went wrong. In 1863 he worked in Port Huron and Stratford. In 1864 he tried Adrian, Michigan; Toledo, Ohio; and Indianapolis, Indiana. The next year took him to Cincinnati, Memphis, and Louisville. Then, in 1866, he traveled south to New Orleans and back again to Louisville.

Moving from one place to another like that may sound exciting. It wasn't. Sometimes Al could get a railroad pass, but often he had to walk. One winter he spent all his money on books and equipment and had to go without an overcoat. His shoes were usually falling apart.

The offices where he worked were small and dirty. Rats snuffled around in the corners and cockroaches joined in whenever the telegraphers stopped work for a meal. At one point Al invented a gadget for electrocuting those unwelcome pets.

Most of the telegraphers lived in cheap rooms, too. That was all they could afford. They made jokes about "the animal kingdom" that shared their rooms.

To take their minds off their troubles, many of the men drank. That never worked for Al. Just a sip of two of whiskey put him to sleep. So he stayed away from the stuff.

Besides, he was already addicted to something far more exciting than alcohol—those everlasting experiments. As he traveled from job to job, Al was learning something about himself. It wasn't telegraphing that he loved. It was all the machinery that went with it. He didn't want to be a telegrapher. He wanted to be an inventor.

Being an inventor took money—money for supplies and equipment and money to live on. And money was one thing Al didn't have. So he had to go on working as a telegrapher and doing experiments on the side.

It was those experiments on the side that often cost him his job. Al simply couldn't be content with doing them on his time off. He had to take them to work. Sometimes he even became annoyed when his job interfered with an experiment.

Telegraphers were supposed to send a signal every half hour to show they were on duty. Al thought that was a waste of time. He invented a gadget that automatically did the half-hour signaling for him. That left him free for reading and experimenting. But when his bosses found out what he was doing, he got into a peck of trouble.

Sometimes he would write down messages and then forget to deliver them. He didn't *mean* to forget. His mind just happened to be busy with a book or a diagram. More than once he told a telegrapher at the other end of the line to hold on a minute. He had just had a good idea and wanted to write it down.

Even worse, though, was the habit he had of taking apart and rewiring the machinery in the office. He wanted to invent a telegraph that could send two messages at the same time on the same wire. Such a machine would cut the cost of telegraphing in half. Al had lots of ideas about how it might be done. But he had to try those ideas out on *something*, didn't he? His bosses didn't see why that something should be their property.

Years later, Al wrote about the disastrous end to one of his jobs:

I went one night into the battery-room to
obtain some sulfuric acid for experimenting.
The carboy tipped over, the acid ran out, went
through the ceiling to the manager's room
below, and ate up his desk and all the carpet.
The next morning I was summoned before him
and told that the company wanted operators,
not experimenters.

One day Al decided to seek his fortune in a far-off land. A
couple of friends told him that telegraphers could earn a lot
of money in Brazil. They were planning to sail to South
America from New Orleans. Did Al want to go with them?

Of course he did.

At once he began to learn Spanish. (Evidently he didn't
know that the Brazilians speak Portuguese.) Then he rushed
home to Port Huron to say good-bye to his family. They
thought that going to Brazil was a terrible idea and told him
so. But that didn't stop Al.

With his two friends he hurried down to New Orleans.
There, as luck would have it, he met a man who had lived in
South America for many years. The man told him how hard
and dangerous a telegrapher's life would be in Brazil. Al
listened carefully—and changed his mind about going.

Later he learned that his two friends had gotten no
farther than Mexico. There they died of yellow fever.

Back home again in Port Huron, Al found his family in sad shape. His sister, Harriet Ann, had died. The house where the Edisons had lived for so many years was about to be taken over by the military. Nancy Edison looked old and sick. Some people said her mind had been affected by all her disappointments. She certainly was disappointed in Al. He didn't seem to be doing a thing with his life.

Well, he thought, maybe he could do better in the East. A friend of his had mentioned the possibility of a job in Boston. Why not try it? He talked the railroad into giving him a free pass and set off again.

He must have been quite a sight when he showed up at the Western Union office in Boston. He wore his hair long under a broad-rimmed hat. His clothes were baggy and rumpled. A plug of tobacco in his cheek made him look as if he had a toothache.

"My peculiar appearance caused much mirth," he said later.

But he got the job.

Boston turned out to be a good place for Al—at least at first. Many people there were interested in inventing and especially in working with electricity.

Before long Al met two of them—Franklin Pope and James Ashley. Al showed them what he had done so far with a machine that could send two messages at once. (It was called a duplex.) Pope and Ashley were impressed and wrote about Al in a newspaper they had helped start, *The Telegrapher*.

Soon Al found himself in a workshop with other young telegrapher-inventors. Ideas seemed to be floating around in the Boston air, just waiting to be grabbed. And Al grabbed his share.

For example, there was the gold ticker. Pope had told Al about stock tickers, which let business people know how stocks were selling at any given time. Why not a system of gold tickers too? It was just what Boston needed. The price of gold was very important to the financial world.

Sure enough, their idea was a success—and did they celebrate!

Meanwhile, Al still was working for Western Union at night. The only sleep he got was catnaps tucked in here and there. Finally he decided to quit his job and work full-time as an inventor.

Several men lent him money to continue work on his duplex and on a better stock ticker. Al threw himself into the projects. He was excited and happy and even managed to invent a vote-recording machine as well. But no one wanted to buy the vote-recording machine and soon things began to go wrong with his other work, too.

One of his projects took him to New York City. Pope let him have a bed and lent him money for food. (Al lived on apple dumplings, pie, and coffee in those days.) The young inventor was feeling discouraged, very discouraged.

But he had no intention of quitting.

"I'll never give up," he wrote to a friend, "for I may have a streak of luck before I die."

Chapter 5

# THE WIZARDS OF THE EAST

Edison's streak of luck seemed to hit soon after he decided to settle in New York. His friend, Franklin Pope, worked for a man called Samuel Laws. Laws had invented the gold ticker that Edison and his friends used in their Boston system. Laws had a complicated master version of that machine in his office at the Gold Indicator Company. It was connected to the offices of three hundred brokers, who paid for the information it sent to them.

One day Edison was watching the machine when suddenly, with a great crash, it stopped. Pope panicked. Laws panicked. The three hundred brokers in their offices panicked and sent three hundred messengers to find out what had gone wrong.

Only Edison kept his head. He looked carefully at the machine. Aha! He could see the problem. A spring had broken and fallen between two gear wheels.

It took a while to get Laws's attention. Finally he was able to tell him what had gone wrong.

"Fix it! Fix it!" cried Laws.

So Edison did and the next day Laws offered him a job.

That began Edison's business connections with the financial wizards of the East. In the years to come, he worked with a great many of them. Sometimes they treated him fairly. Sometimes they didn't. Sometimes they drove him crazy and he called them "small-brained capitalists." Sometimes he drove them crazy and they called him "a harebrained inventor."

A few people thought that inventors such as Edison were "captive scientists." The financial wizards owned them and forced them to perform like trained monkeys, said those people. But Edison didn't really care about all that. The ins and outs, the battles and truces of the financial world didn't interest him. All he was interested in was their machines. As long as the wizards let him invent things—and paid him for them—he was happy.

When Laws sold the Gold Indicator Company, Edison set up a partnership with Pope and Ashley. Pope and Edison were the electrical engineers in the new business, which they called Pope, Edison, and Company. They built "various types of electrical devices and apparatus," set up private telegraph lines, and made and tested scientific instruments. Ashley gave them free advertising space in *The Telegrapher*.

Before long, Edison had invented a special kind of telegraph called a gold printer. It told the price of both gold and silver. Pope, Edison, and Company made the machines and rented them to importers and currency dealers.

This made Western Union nervous. The new little company was stealing away its customers. So Western Union bought the gold printer service for fifteen thousand dollars. Edison's share was five thousand. It was the most money he had ever made at once.

Usually he spent money as fast as he made it—mostly on equipment. But he was worried about his parents and wanted to help them.

> DEAR FATHER AND MOTHER,
>
> I sent you another express package saturday, enclosed you will find the receipt for the same.
>
> I C Edison writes me that mother is not very well and that you have to work very hard. I guess you had better take it easy after this. Don't do any hard work and get mother anything she desires. You can draw on me for money. Write me and say how much money you will need till June and I will send the amount on the first of that month. Give love to all folks. and write me the town-news. . . .
>
> > Your affec. son
> > THOMAS A.

Edison's punctuation was rather bad. But his heart was definitely in the right place.

In the months ahead he came up with a number of inventions. Most of them were little things that improved the telegraph. After a while, though, he tired of the partnership with Pope and Ashley. He was doing all the work, but he had to divide the profits equally with them. That didn't seem quite fair. So when Western Union offered to hire him as an inventor, Edison jumped at the chance.

Soon he was hard at work on a new project. Many stockbrokers used tickers hitched up to a central ticker like the one Laws had in his office. But sometimes the brokers' tickers went wild and spit out crazy figures. Edison's job was to invent a device that would bring the outside tickers back into line with the central ticker.

He did it and the financial wizards were amazed.

His boss, General Marshall Lefferts, asked him how much he thought Western Union should pay him for the device.

Edison didn't know. He'd like five thousand dollars. But that might be too much. He should say three thousand.

"General, suppose you make me an offer," he said at last.

"How would forty thousand dollars strike you?" asked Lefferts.

It struck him very well indeed.

The next day he signed a contract and received a check. Off rushed Edison to the bank. But when he handed the check to a teller, the man "yelled out a large amount of jargon."

Poor Edison had never been in a bank before. He didn't understand a word the man said. Back he trudged to Western Union, certain he had been cheated out of his forty thousand dollars.

When he told people there what had happened, they laughed. Hadn't he ever cashed a check before? (He hadn't.) Didn't he know he had to endorse it? (He didn't.)

General Lefferts's secretary went back to the bank with him. This time Edison signed his name on the back of the check before handing it over. Then the teller gave him his money—all in ten- and twenty-dollar bills. There were so many bills that Edison had to stuff them all through his clothing.

Looking rather lumpy, he went home to the boardinghouse in Newark, New Jersey, where he lived at the time. Instead of celebrating his good luck, he sat up alone all night in his room. He was terrified that some burgler would break in and murder him for all that money.

The next day, some friends told him about savings accounts. So Edison returned to the same bank and deposited most of his money. Now he could sleep again.

And this was the same man who invented machines that amazed the financial wizards of the East.

Next Edison was supposed to set up small factories to make stock tickers for Western Union. He found two places in Newark. Then he began to buy equipment and hire mechanics. It was an important job for someone who was only twenty-four years old.

But that didn't worry him. Instead he worried about his mother. Friends and family wrote about her poor health. He wanted to see her. But he was just too busy with the factories to get away.

Then, in April of 1871, he received a telegram. His mother had died two days before. Edison returned home for her funeral. For a few minutes he knelt quietly by her grave. Then he hurried back to Newark. His heart was sore, but it wouldn't hurt quite so much, he thought, if he could bury himself in hard work.

And bury himself he did. As far as work went, he was doing what he had always wanted to do—inventing machines and building them. The people who worked with him made the job even better—John Ott, who could put anything mechanical together; Charles Batchelor, an Englishman with a black beard; John Kruesi, a former clock maker from Switzerland; and Sigmund Bergmann, from Germany. These men loved and understood machines as much as Edison did.

Then there was Miss Mary Stilwell. She was just sixteen years old and had the loveliest golden hair. Her job was to punch holes in telegraph tape. A number of other women worked with her. But somehow Edison always found himself watching her.

One day he smiled at her and said, "What do you think of me, little girl? Do you like me?"

"Why Mr. Edison, you frighten me," stammered poor Mary. "That is—I—"

"Don't be in a hurry about telling me," said Edison kindly. "It doesn't matter much, unless you would like to marry me."

Later he wrote more about his romance in his diary.

> Even in my courtship my deafness was a help. In the first place it excused me for getting quite a little closer to her than I would have dared . . . to hear what she said. If something had not overcome my natural bashfulness I might have been too faint of heart to win. And after things were going nicely, I found hearing unnecessary.

She *did* want to marry Mr. Edison, decided Mary. But her parents said they must wait a year because she was so young. In spite of that, the couple was married just a few weeks later, on Christmas Day, 1871. Edison had bought a house on Wright Street in Newark and after the wedding luncheon, he took his bride to their new home.

They hadn't been there five minutes before he asked Mary if she would mind if he went down to the factory for a while. He had this idea, you see, about the stock tickers. . . .

Of course he must go, said Mary.

Later, *he* always claimed that he returned home by dinner time. But a family legend disagreed. According to that legend, he was still hard at work when a friend rushed into the lab and asked what on earth he was doing there.

"What time is it?" asked Edison.

"Midnight," said his friend.

"Is that so?" said Edison. "I must go home then. I was married today."

Fortunately, the newlyweds left the next day for a honeymoon at Niagara Falls—a safe distance away from that tempting laboratory.

Finally Edison had found a happy life. A year after their wedding, he and Mary had a baby girl, named Marion. In 1876 they had a little boy, Thomas Junior. (Edison called his daughter Dot and his son Dash—in honor of Morse code.) A second boy, William Leslie, was born in 1878. (He didn't seem to receive a telegraphic nickname.)

Mary Edison never did understand much about her husband's work. Maybe she didn't want to understand. After all, it was *him* she cared about. And for Thomas Edison that was just as well. Now he had a place to get away from work—at least for a little while.

Chapter 6

# MONEY TROUBLES

It was a good thing that Edison was happy at home, because suddenly he found himself in trouble at work.

As a boy he had hated math. When he grew up, he hated bookkeeping just as much. So he didn't keep any financial books. He stuck his bills on a hook. When the sender of a particular bill complained loudly enough, he paid him.

It was no way to run a business.

But Edison refused to be bothered by such details. Soon after the birth of his daughter, postal authorities in England invited him to visit. They were interested in buying the rights to some of his inventions.

So, armed with three boxes of equipment, Edison set sail in April of 1873 on a ship called *The Jumping Java*.

His trip lasted six weeks. On the whole, it was a flop. The English were very impressed with his work; but they didn't buy anything. Besides, the food was so bad that his "imagination was getting into a coma." Finally he found a French pastry shop. That got him through the rest of his visit.

He returned home to find Mary wringing her hands and the sheriff pounding at his door. Edison's nonexistent bookkeeping finally had caught up with him. He owed money to so many people that the sheriff threatened to close his factories and sell his machinery and equipment.

He couldn't have chosen a worse time to get into trouble. The whole country was suffering from an economic depression. The financial wizards wouldn't even talk to him. Only his friend and partner, Joseph Murray, would lend him enough money to keep him going for a while.

What should he do now? Edison wondered. He could think of just one answer: go on inventing.

First he came up with a signal box. People could use it to alert a messenger service in case of fire, burglars, sudden illness, or some other emergency in their homes. The signal box brought him a few thousand dollars. But it didn't begin to solve his financial problems.

So he invented an electric pen. It worked from a small, battery-operated motor and could be used to make several copies of a document quickly.

He also invented "a device for multiplying copies of letters called the Mimeograph." That invention he sold to the A.B. Dick Company.

Surely with those three inventions—plus many less important ones—his money troubles should be over.

But they weren't. New inventions don't always become popular overnight. It takes a while for people to realize how useful they can be. Meanwhile, Edison was struggling to stay afloat.

What he really wanted to concentrate on was the telegraph. At that time Western Union owned the patents to a duplex telegraph invented by J.B. Stearns. It didn't work too well. Besides, it could send only two messages at the same time in *opposite* directions.

Edison thought he could improve the Stearns machine with one that would send two or more messages at the same time in the *same* direction.

It is not unusual for several inventors to be working on similar projects. Sometimes they even borrow ideas from one another. But they usually end up with slightly different results. Their patents make these differences their own property—unless they sell the patents.

William Orton, president of Western Union, had been allowing Edison to work with telegraphs in his company even before Edison went to England. In return, Edison had made some improvements in the duplex. But now his financial problems made it more and more difficult for him to work.

At one point he even became ill.

"I have been sick in bed," he wrote. "Have had the most interesting features of four thousand nightmares in the daytime. Cause: root beer and duplex."

At last, though, all his work seemed about to pay off. He invented a quadruplex telegraph that could send two messages in one direction and two in another, all at the same time and on the same wire. *That* should make Western Union happy.

He also invented a relay device for the Atlantic & Pacific Telegraph Company. It saved the firm from going out of business.

But those were the days of the "robber barons." Leaders of big businesses did almost anything they liked—and got away with it. Laws to make them behave more honestly didn't come until later.

So Atlantic & Pacific paid Edison only part of what it owed him. And Western Union dragged its feet about paying him at all.

Edison was desperate. Something, he decided, was better than nothing. So he took his quadruplex to Jay Gould, head of Atlantic & Pacific, and sold it to him. Again Gould gave him just part of the money he had earned.

Western Union was furious. It wanted that quadruplex. Soon a court battle raged between the two companies. It lasted almost seven years. In the end, Jay Gould had taken over Western Union, but Edison was no better off than before.

"When Gould got the Western Union," he wrote, "I knew no further progress in telegraphy was possible, and I went into other lines."

One of those "other lines" was experiments with some strange sparks he had seen. We know now they were electricity, moving so fast that they couldn't be measured with equipment of that time.

But Edison thought they might be a whole new force. He called it "etheric force" or "etheric current."

His discovery had the whole world of science on its toes for a while. But then the excitement died down and Edison lost interest in the sparks. They weren't really his kind of work. Anyway, his mind was busy with a new idea.

He was sick and tired of business and all the headaches that went with it. What he wanted now was to live with his family and assistants in some quiet place and do nothing but invent. At last he had a little money put aside. Why not build that perfect spot he kept dreaming about?

He sent his father to Menlo Park, New Jersey. There Sam Edison supervised the building of a huge, barnlike structure. Menlo Park was a tiny town, about twenty-five miles from New York City, with only six houses. No one would bother the inventors there except pigs and cows. And Edison had a fence put up to keep them out.

Menlo Park was the ideal place for a research center—for, that is, Edison's new idea for a research center. There already were research centers at universities. But he didn't intend to do any teaching. There were also research centers that experimented with no special goals in mind. But Edison intended to deal with specifics.

His idea was for a brand-new kind of research center—

one that did *practical* research. Companies would come to him and tell him what they needed. Then he and his assistants would invent it. But they would do their work far away from the noise and bother of the business world.

As soon as the large building was completed, Edison moved his equipment into it. He bought a farmhouse next to the building for Mary and the children. (He knew already that he wouldn't be spending much time at home. But he wanted home to be nearby.) Two of his assistants bought other houses in town. The rest moved into Mrs. Jordan's boardinghouse.

Before long, Menlo Park became known as "Edison Village." It turned out to be the place where Edison lived some of the happiest years of his life.

Chapter 7

# A NEW WIZARD

"The care and anxieties of being an inventor seemed more than flesh and blood can stand."

Alexander Graham Bell, inventor of the telephone, wrote those words in 1875, not long before Edison settled in at Menlo Park. A year earlier, Edison might have agreed with Bell. Now he probably wouldn't have. He was tremendously happy.

In a burst of good spirits, he gave his new address to a friend:

". . . at Menlo Park, Western Div., Globe, Planet Earth, Middlesex Country [sic], four miles from Rahway, the prettiest spot in New Jersey, on the Penna. Railway, on a High Hill."

There was absolutely nothing to do for entertainment in the town. Sometimes Mary Edison found that depressing. But not Edison and his coworkers. They just invented and then invented some more. They began work at seven in the morning and often went on working all night. (When that happened, Mary sent over a midnight snack.)

"We don't pay anything and we work all the time," Edison once told a young man who was looking for a job.

The young man took the job. What did he care about long hours and poor pay? There was magic at Menlo Park and he wanted to be a part of it.

Even Edison's children saw some of the magic. When she was a small girl, Marion (Dot) loved to play at her father's feet as he worked in the laboratory. Sometimes he made mechanical toys for her and Dash—toys no other children in the world had.

One of the toys was a little paper man with a funnel on top of his head. When Marion shouted into the funnel, gears were set in motion and the little man sawed wood.

But Edison and his coworkers were interested in far more than toys. They wanted to invent a speaking telegraph. William Orton was still president of Western Union at the time and he encouraged Edison on the project. In spite of his past problems with Western Union, Edison agreed.

Once again, many inventors were busy attacking the same problem. It's easy now to look back and see where they would all end up. But those men couldn't look back. They had to work in the present and fight their way through to an answer.

Alexander Graham Bell won that fight. He invented the telephone. On February 14, 1876, he filed for his patent.

Bell's early phone was far from perfect, though. It didn't have enough power to transmit voices loudly and clearly. So Edison began to work at making a better telephone.

At last he saw the problem. Bell's phone had a good sound receiver. But it didn't have a good transmitter. It needed both to be useful.

Edison decided to invent that transmitter. He also would figure out a way to give it enough power so voices could be carried for long distances.

A lot of problems went with this project. Patiently, Edison and his assistants solved them one at a time. For example, something had to be done about sibilant consonants, especially *s*'s. They could make a sentence sound like a nest of snakes if the transmitter weren't right.

"Physicists and Sphynxes in majestical Mists," the men said into their machine again and again until each word came out crisp and clear.

Working with the problem of good sound was even more difficult for Edison than for other people. After all, he was almost deaf. But he plugged along for his transmitter.

Alexander Graham Bell had offered to sell the patents on his telephone to Western Union a couple of years earlier. The company wasn't interested. It couldn't see that in the long run the telephone would be far more practical than the speaking telegraph Western Union thought it wanted.

By 1878 Western Union had changed its mind. But it was too late. Bell had found other people with money to back him. The Bell Telephone Company already was in business.

Still, it didn't have Edison's transmitter, which really did improve the telephone. So Western Union set up another company, the American Speaking Telephone Company, and began to compete with Bell.

The battle got rough, especially when the Bell Company found someone to invent its own transmitter.

"It's too much like Edison's!" shouted Western Union.

"Our man filed for a patent first!" replied the Bell Company.

That battle sizzled in the courts for fifteen years.

Edison understood exactly what was going on. "The Western Union [was] pirating the Bell receiver, and the Boston company [Bell] was pirating the Western Union transmitter."

In the end, both (or neither) sides won. The courts ruled that Edison's patent for the transmitter was valid. But Western Union pulled out of the telephone business and sold its lines to Bell.

Long before that happened, though, Edison was supposed to be paid for his work. Orton asked how much he wanted. Edison had been in this position before. He told Orton to make an offer. He hoped the offer would be at least twenty-five thousand dollars.

Orton offered a hundred thousand.

Fine, said Edison coolly. But pay me six thousand a year for seventeen years. He understood himself well by then. If he received the money all at once, chances were he would spend it all at once.

The battle between Western Union and Bell in the United States had not ended before the new one broke out in England. This time it was between Bell and the Edison Telephone Company of Great Britain, Limited.

Edison thought he would have a better chance of winning in England if he invented a new receiver. So he did—and the fight went on. Finally the two companies decided to merge.

All in all, Edison earned about a quarter of a million dollars for his work on the telephone. He was able to leave that area of research in a very good mood and move on to other things.

Some of his projects during those early years at Menlo Park included electric pens and mimeographs, instruments to measure sound, and improvements in the telegraph and submarine cable. He and his assistants also did research in chemicals and drugs, which they sometimes used in their inventions.

But most exciting of all was the phonograph. Edison invented it almost by accident. While working on his telegraph recorder, he had heard funny noises. They sounded to him somewhat like human voices. That got him interested.

At first he worked with waxed paper and a device with a blunt pin attached. He pulled the paper through the device and shouted "Halloo!" When he pulled it through again, "we heard a distinct sound, which a strong imagination might have translated into the original 'Halloo!' "

For four more months he worked. But still wasn't thinking about a phonograph. He was trying to invent a telephone repeater. Business people could use it, he figured, to record and save telephone conversations.

At last he switched from waxed paper to a grooved cylinder covered with tinfoil. John Kruesi, the Swiss clock maker, made the machine, although Edison designed it. Kruesi thought the whole idea was absurd, but he did his part.

Then, on December 6, 1877, came the moment of testing. Edison cranked the handle of the machine and shouted into it, "Mary had a little lamb. . . ." When he finished the rhyme, he played it back. And there it was, clear as day: "Mary had a little lamb. . . ."

Later, Edison described his feelings. "I was never so taken aback in all my life," he said. "Everybody was astonished. I was always afraid of things that worked the first time."

From then on, the phonograph was pure fun for him. No one could believe it. Everyone wanted to see and hear it. Visitors flocked to Menlo Park. Across the Atlantic, England, Scotland, and France cheered the phonograph.

Sometimes the proud young inventor was accused of being a wizard. A bishop visited him and snooped all around the laboratory, looking for the ventriloquist who made the machine talk.

Edison didn't mind. It was a nice change to have folks

think he was a wizard. Better than being called "hare-brained" anyway!

Enchanted audiences watched him pat his invention and ask, "Well, old phonograph, how are we getting on down there?" Then he would crank it up and it would talk back to him.

One group of scientists heard it say, "The speaking phonograph had the honor of presenting itself before the American Academy of Sciences."

The phonograph even got invited—along with Edison—to the White House. *Everyone* was wild about it, including its inventor.

"This is my baby," he told a newspaper reporter, "and I expect it to grow up and be a big feller and support me in my old age."

He had some good ideas as to how it could be used. It could record letters without a secretary, "read" books to the blind, teach people to speak better, and act as a family scrapbook of voices. Tiny phonographs could be used to make talking dolls for children. Teachers could record instructions—and maybe even spelling words—for their pupils. Clocks could tell folks the time of day—out loud. And the phonograph could definitely be used to record and play back music.

It's amazing how many of these dreams eventually came true. But first the new machine needed a lot of work. Tinfoil "records" didn't last long, the quality of sound was far from great, and cranking a handle wasn't the best means of making a recording.

Edison thought of several ways to improve his invention. But then, all of a sudden, he put it aside—for ten years.

Maybe he got bored with it. Or maybe he was tired of all these visitors interrupting his work. *They* might think he was a wizard, but *he* knew better.

Much later he said, "Genius is 1 percent inspiration and 99 percent perspiration." (He also wrote, "There is no substitute for hard work.")

Besides, another idea began tugging at his mind during that summer of 1878. It had to do with darkness—and with light.

## Chapter 8

# TOWARD THE LIGHT

Edison had been working long and hard. During the spring of 1878, he became ill from overwork. He hadn't had a real vacation since his honeymoon seven years earlier.

But by summer he perked up again. He invented a device he called a microtasimeter. It could measure tiny changes in temperature and might be used, he thought, to show how much heat the stars gave off.

On July 23, a total eclipse of the sun would be visible in the Rocky Mountains. Two professors, Charles F. Young and Rufus Brackett, who were going out to see it, wanted to take a microtasimeter along.

After Edison finished one for them, two more professors showed up. George F. Barker and Henry Draper wanted a microtasimeter, too. Furthermore, they offered to take Edison along to the Rockies.

That was an offer too good to refuse. He really had no business going. Mary was pregnant with their third child and feeling ill. Edison himself was supposed to be working on other projects.

But he wanted a vacation—badly. So he finished another microtasimeter and left.

After more than a week of dusty train travel, he and the professors arrived in Rawlins, Wyoming. Edison was delighted. This was cowboy country!

He wandered over to the local jail and peered in at a real horse thief and a real train robber. A real gunslinger barged into his room one night. The gunman, known as Texas Jack, wanted to meet the man who had invented the phonograph.

On the day of the eclipse Edison and his friends set up their equipment. Unfortunately, the microtasimeter didn't work very well. It was too sensitive. It measured *all* heat, including the body heat of the men using it.

For once, though, Edison wasn't too depressed about a scientific failure. He was having a glorious time.

After the eclipse, he and the professors took a hunting and fishing trip. Then they traveled on to California. Edison decided to get an uninterrupted view as the train chugged through the mountains. He asked railroad officials if he could ride on the cowcatcher on the front of the locomotive.

The train engineers advised one safety device. It was going to be a bumpy ride. So Edison sat on a cushion atop the cowcatcher for his first glimpse of some glorious Western landscapes.

All in all, the vacation lasted two months. Of course Edison spent part of that time discussing science. Some of the best conversations were with Professor Barker. Barker was interested in using electricity to provide light. Would Edison like to do some research in that area?

"Just at that time I wanted to take up something new," Edison wrote later.

As a matter of fact, he already had played around with the idea a bit. He had been fascinated by arc lights—carbon rods that burned by electricity generated by a dynamo.

So, after he got back from his trip, he began to study electricity and lighting more carefully. He did it the same way he always looked into things. He wrote:

> When I want to discover something, I begin by reading up everything that has been done along that line in the past—that's what all these books in the library are for. I see what has been accomplished at great labor and expense in the past. I gather the data of many thousands of experiments as a starting point, and then I make thousands more.

Before he began those "thousands more" experiments, though, he visited an arc light factory in Ansonia, Connecticut. It was owned by William Wallace and Moses Farmer.

Wallace gave him a warm welcome and invited him to snoop around to his heart's content. He trusted Edison not to steal any ideas.

Edison roamed all over the place, getting more excited by

the minute. But it wasn't the arc lights that thrilled him. He didn't really think arc lights were the answer. They were too bright to be used to light private homes.

No, there had to be something better than arc light. And he thought he had a glimmering of what it might be.

"I believe I can beat you making electric light," he told Wallace. "I do not think you are working in the right direction."

Then he rushed home and began to experiment.

As he worked, visions of the future spun through Edison's mind. One day soon there would be a whole electrical industry! Its giant dynamos would run machinery during the day and light homes at night.

The gas industry could forget about lighting and concentrate on heating and cooking. Gas had never been good for lighting, anyway. It was dirty, dangerous, and unreliable.

Yes, electric lighting was the way of the future. But not the harsh glow of arc lights. Surely there must be some way to harness electricity's power, to break the light down into smaller parts.

He was not dealing with just one invention, Edison soon realized. He was going to have to come up with a whole raft of them. Lamps to contain the light. Lamp holders. Better dynamos. Meters to measure the electricity used. Switches. And on and on and on.

He would never need the rest of those things if he didn't

have the lamp. So he decided to start there.

First he tried burning a strip of carbon in a jar with a partial vacuum. It burned for about eight minutes. Not even long enough to get through the evening paper. So forget carbon.

Next he tried burning different kinds of metal wire. Platinum seemed to do best. But it also melted. So Edison invented a device to make the wire blink off for just an instant. The blink was enough to cool it so it wouldn't melt.

But he wasn't really happy with that answer. So he went on trying other materials and mixtures of materials.

Meanwhile, Edison could see he would need more money to go on experimenting and to try out his inventions once they were completed. In fact, he'd need a *lot* of money. Again he would have to turn to the financial wizards of the East, but now he knew how to handle them.

Breezily he told reporters from the *New York Sun, Herald,* and *Tribune* that he was very close to his goal. Soon he could light up all of downtown New York with 500,000 incandescent lamps and a few dynamos!

He was talking through his hat.

But when the wizards heard such words, they sniffed the air and smelled money. So by mid-October of 1878, Edison had all the backers he needed and the Edison Electric Light Company was born.

Now, if he could just get the lamp invented!

Other people joined the race. Whoever came up with that lamp would earn a lot of money. Edison's own arrangement with his backers would make him a millionaire.

So on he worked, in spite of a short bout of sickness. All he needed, he thought, was the right filament that would burn in a vacuum.

He experimented with platinum, chromium, molybdenum, osmium, boron, silicon, nickel, and platinum again. He found a pump that created a better vacuum. He learned how to seal the bulbs. Slowly but steadily he was making progress.

But he moved too slowly for some of his backers. How much more money for experimenting would be needed before he came up with something? A visit to Menlo Park didn't do much to calm their nerves. It seemed to them that he had a long way to go.

On he struggled. Maybe platinum wasn't the right substance after all. What about . . . carbon! That was where he had started and that just might be where he would end up.

In October of 1879 Edison and his assistants were working round the clock. Carbonized thread seemed to burn best; so they made a filament from it. Edison later wrote:

We built the lamp and turned on the current. It lit up, and in the first breathless minutes we measured its resistance quickly and found it was 275 ohms—all we wanted. Then we sat down and looked at that lamp. We wanted to see how long it would burn. The problem was solved—if the filament would last. The day was—let me see—October 21, 1879.

We sat and looked and the lamp continued to burn, and the longer it burned the more fascinated we were. None of us could go to bed, and there was no sleep for any of us for forty hours. We sat and just watched it with anxiety growing into elation.

It lasted about forty-five hours, and then I said, 'If it will burn that number of hours now, I know I can make it burn a hundred.'

But the battle wasn't over yet. The carbonized thread, Edison decided, wasn't quite right after all.

He tried many substances, including celluloid, coconut hair and coconut shell, different kinds of drawing paper, different kinds of wood shavings, fishing line, cork, and flax. He even tried a few hairs from the beard of one of his assistants. (They worked pretty well, but the supply was limited.)

Then, finally, he tried a strip of tough, carbonized cardboard. It worked. The bulbs burned up to 170 hours.

Exhausted but triumphant, Edison filed for his patent. The date was November 1, 1879.

Above: A recreation of the Menlo Park compound now can be seen in Greenfield Village, Dearborn, Michigan. Below: Edison (in the center wearing a chemist's cap) and his staff inside the lab at Menlo Park.

Edison had quite an elaborate laboratory for the times.

In 1878, Edison displayed his phonograph in Washington, D.C.

A newspaper advertisement, in German, for Edison's "Gem."

Thomas Edison works on a filament for his electric lamp while Henry Ford and Francis Jehl watch.

Edison's laboratory in West Orange, New Jersey around 1900

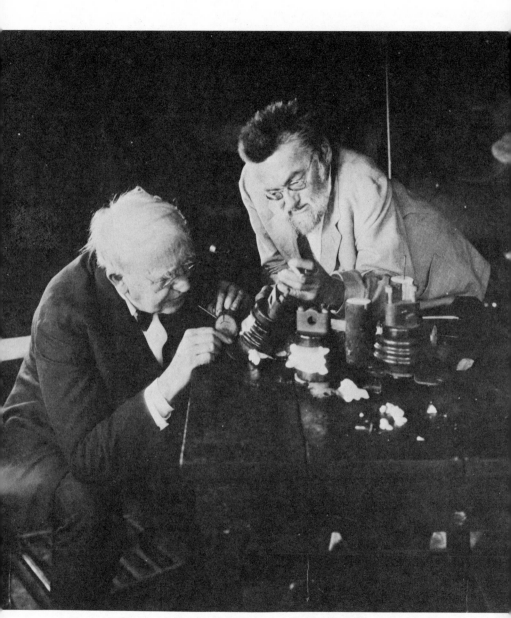

Thomas Edison and Charles Steinmetz, an electrical engineer, in Edison's
laboratory at Schenectady, New York, in October of 1922.

Henry Ford talking
to Edison

Below: The "Black Maria,"
the world's first motion
picture studio, was
erected in 1893 on the
grounds of Edison's
laboratory in West
Orange, New Jersey.

Thomas Edison and friends on a camping trip at an old grist mill in West Virginia in 1918. Left to right are Edison, Harvey S. Firestone, Jr.; John Burroughs, naturalist; Henry Ford, and Harvey S. Firestone, organizer of Firestone Tire and Rubber Company; seated is R.J.H. De Loach.

Edison with some of his lamps

Chapter 9

# ALL HE PROMISED

What is it? neighbors of Menlo Park asked one another during that late fall of 1879.

What's going on? wondered passengers on night trains passing through the village.

Before long the truth sank in. Edison had invented an electric lamp! Furthermore, he and a coworker, Francis Upton, were using electric lamps to light their homes.

Surely the financial wizards must be dancing for joy on Wall Street. Surely they must be tumbling over one another to give Edison more money to go on with his work.

Wrong.

Those wizards had to think the situation over very carefully. Was Edison's invention a moneymaker? Or just another laboratory toy?

Patiently Edison tried to explain that he *did* have a moneymaker for them. But it wouldn't make money unless he had more funds to continue his work. The electric lamp was just the first big step. The next one: a power station right there at Menlo Park.

But the wizards still dithered until one of Edison's friends, Grosvenor Lowrey, took matters into his own hands. Enough of secrecy, he decided. What the financial backers needed was a good shot of publicity to bring them to their senses.

So he leaked the news to the *New York Herald*. The headline screamed:

### EDISON'S LIGHT.
### The Great Inventor's Triumph
### in Electric Illumination

Furthermore, said another announcement, Edison would celebrate New Year's Eve by lighting the area around Menlo Park.

He would? thought Edison. Who came up with that idea? He wasn't ready to do any such thing. But he decided to do the best he could.

All week visitors poured into Menlo Park. On New Year's Eve, 1879, three thousand of them milled around in great excitement. They weren't disappointed. True, Edison had only about forty electric lamps scattered around his laboratory and grounds. But forty electric lights looked impressive to those eager visitors. Besides, most of them also got to see the great man himself.

Some of those who milled around with the crowd on New Year's Eve were not very impressed.

It's a trick! cried one inventor whom Edison had beaten. (The poor man was very drunk.)

Disappointing! sneered men from gas companies. (But

inside they were probably quaking. If electricity worked, what would happen to gaslights?)

One man, an electrician, tried to short-circuit the whole display. He failed and Edison's guards marched him out of the area.

There were also many people who hadn't the slightest idea what was going on, but who were excited about it anyway.

One confused fellow just couldn't figure out how Mr. Edison had gotten that red-hot hairpin (the filament) into the bottle (the bulb).

A curious lady bent over a generator to see how it worked. Suddenly she felt her hair falling down around her ears. The magnetic force of the generator had pulled out all her hairpins.

Best of all, though, the tight fists of the financial wizards uncurled. They gave Edison the money he needed to go on with the project.

A railroad and shipping tycoon, Henry Villard, also gave him a chance to try out his ideas in a practical way. Villard had a large ship, the S.S. *Columbia*, set to sail down around Cape Horn and on to California. Could Edison light it with electricity?

Edison built four dynamos for the *Columbia*'s engine room. He strung 115 lamps all over the ship. Glowing like a Christmas tree, she steamed off down Delaware Bay.

Two months later she arrived in San Francisco. During

all that time, not even a single bulb had failed.

But Edison was still not satisfied with his filament. Once again he began to search for a better material. Macaroni? Onion rind? Pomegranate peel?

Bamboo!

Suddenly Edison found himself very excited about bamboo. He wanted to study samples of it from all over the world. He sent explorers to China and Japan, the West Indies, Central and South America, India, Ceylon, and Burma. They tramped through jungles and rain forests, caught fevers, and fought off wild animals. But they brought back bamboo—six thousand different species of it.

And the financial wizards meekly paid for all their travels.

Meanwhile, a number of other people still hoped to beat Edison to the electric industry of which he dreamed.

Two men from San Francisco, named Molera and Cebrian, thought they could make arc lights work in private homes. Put the lights on the stairs, they said, and bounce their light off mirrors and through holes into the rooms. It was not exactly a practical idea.

In England, a man named Joseph Swan did better work. He came up with some of Edison's answers—all on his own. But he failed to protect his work by filing for patents.

Elihu Thomson and Edwin Houston went on working with arc lights. They also improved dynamos. Thomson and

Houston even formed their own company, the American Electric Company. It started out small, but later gave Edison trouble.

A number of cities, including Philadelphia, Cleveland, San Francisco, and New York, ordered arc lights from still another group, the Brush Electric Company. Their lights, mounted on tall iron poles, lit up certain streets, stores, and hotels.

The gas company owners went on sneering.

And once again Edison's wizards grew restless.

But Edison ignored them all. He had found the right kind of bamboo for his filament and was busy with ideas for the *distribution* of electric power. Not only did his plan for distribution have to work—it had to work *cheaply* or no one would want to use it.

The only way for cheap distribution, as far as he could see, was *multiple* distribution. A city would be divided into districts, each district with its own power plant. Within each district there would be main lines carrying large loads of electricity, with smaller feeder lines in other places.

Getting to that point, though, involved a lot of inventing. Edison took out sixty patents in 1880 alone. When he needed to relax, he turned away from electric lighting and worked on another project—an electric train.

But this wasn't a little toy electric train like those that run around Christmas trees. It was *big*—it ran outside and had a six-foot-long locomotive and an open-air passenger car.

A toy for the children? No, at first it was a toy for Edison himself. Soon he began to see it was far more than a toy. Oh, yes, it had bugs—like jumping off the track and a nasty, burning smell. But those bugs could be worked out and then. . . .

Edison's friend Henry Villard gave him money to continue his work. Eventually, though, Edison put aside the electric train idea. He simply had too much else to do and his other financial backers were howling again.

The outdoor display had worked well the first time. Why not try it again? This time it would be on a much bigger scale. He couldn't exactly set up streetlights, since Menlo Park had no streets. But he could put lamp posts where streets *might* have been.

Furthermore, he would run his power lines underground so they wouldn't clutter up the sky like everyone else's. Insulation for those lines? One of his men promptly invented it—a foul-smelling mixture of asphalt, oxidized linseed oil, parafin, and beeswax.

Then Edison started working on a bigger, better dynamo to be hooked up directly to a huge steam engine. He wasn't sure he could make the New Year's Eve deadline, but at least his backers seemed happy and excited again.

On December 20, 1880, a group of New York politicians traveled to Menlo Park for a preview showing. Edison let them see his phonograph and his loud-speaking telephone as well as the lighting system. But the men didn't really understand what they were looking at. They just stood around, yawning and shuffling their feet, until refreshments were served. Then they perked up.

"Speech! Speech!" they yelled. Their mouths dropped open when they finally realized which of the men was Edison. To their surprise he looked just like a regular fellow!

A few days later, the "regular fellow" lit up hundreds of outdoor lights to amaze and astonish the public. The new steam engine hadn't arrived in time, so he couldn't do the thing as planned. But it was a grand show anyway.

"In every direction stretched out long lines of electric lights, whose lustre made wide white circles on the white-clad earth," wrote a reporter for the *New York Herald.* "One could not tire of gazing at those starry lines."

In January the steam engine finally arrived and Edison connected it to his big dynamo. Together the pair made a powerful rumpus. But they worked. Edison ordered six more engines and began to think about the Pearl Street district in New York City. That was where he planned to do his first large-scale wiring.

The Pearl Street area was perfect for his purposes. It had private homes and small factories. Best of all, it had the offices and banks of the financial wizards. They had spent their money. Now they would see what they were getting for it.

It took some clever work to get a franchise from the city for the project. Two of his wily backers managed that. Edison moved to New York to supervise the installation of the power plant.

Meanwhile, he had run into another problem. He needed factories to make bulbs, switches, dynamos, and all the other equipment that would make his system work. Such factories would cost money, and suddenly the backers wouldn't cough it up.

Later Edison explained:

> Wall Street could not see its way clear to finance a new and untried business. We were confronted by a stupendous obstacle. Nowhere in the world could we obtain any of the items or devices necessary for the exploitation of the system. The directors of the Edison Electric Light Company would not go into manufacturing. Thus forced to the wall, I was forced to go into the manufacturing business myself.

He had to sell much of his stock to raise money for the factories. And how pleased he must have been when his coworkers pitched in to help.

The Edison Lamp Company was founded by Thomas Edison, Charles Batchelor, Francis Upton, and Edward Johnson. Sigmund Bergmann organized a company to make fuses, switches, and similar devices. John Kruesi ran the Electric Tube Company. A young man from England, Samuel Insull, helped Edison with financial problems.

Headquarters for Edison was a mansion on Fifth Avenue—and did he love it! He spent almost all his time there, while his family lived in a hotel and rarely saw him. (Maybe they were used to his absences by then. Everyone had noticed for a long time that Edison's work was his real family.)

He bought old buildings and had them turned into a power station. Dig up the streets and lay mains and feeders, he ordered. His various factories hummed and switches, lines, and all the rest came pouring out.

At the same time, some of Edison's men were setting up equipment to light a district in London. The London project was finished first and was a tremendous success.

But there was a lot more still to be done in New York. Edison had three Jumbo dynamos installed at the Pearl Street station. On July 6, 1882, they were given a test run. It was awful. The Jumbos made terrifying noises and showered the room with sparks and flames. Some of the workmen ran from the station.

Fortunately Edison and another man managed to turn the monsters off. What had gone wrong? After looking at several solutions, Edison decided that what he needed was different steam engines.

So work went on. Tests were made. Last-minute inventions were invented. Finally, on September 4, 1882, everything seemed ready.

For once Edison didn't want a lot of publicity—not until he was certain the system would work. His plan was to start by turning on the lights at the Wall Street offices of J.P. Morgan, one of his backers. Morgan was to invite the other backers to gather with him in his office at three o'clock.

Reporters found out what was going on after all. Maybe they saw Edison arrive at his power station that morning in a frock coat and a white derby. (That was *not* his usual way of dressing.) But they didn't see him roll up his sleeves to check out the equipment one last time. He wouldn't let them in. Not, he said, until after three o'clock.

At last he left the station and went to Morgan's office. With him were Kruesi, Upton, Johnson, Bergmann, and Insull. His chief engineer, John Lieb, stayed behind to throw the switch. Since there was no telephone connection between the power station and Morgan's office, Edison and Lieb had synchronized their watches. They wanted the timing to be perfect.

"A hundred dollars the lights don't go on," said one of the doubting wizards.

"Taken," said Edison. He flicked the switch. The lights came on.

How the wizards shouted and marveled then. But not

Edison. At one of the proudest moments of his life, he simply said, "I have accomplished all I promised."

# Chapter 10

# BAD TIMES, GOOD TIMES

The peaceful days at Menlo Park had ended. Edison was firmly dug in at his Fifth Avenue headquarters. His family had moved to an apartment near Gramercy Park. They still occasionally used the house at Menlo Park for a summer home. But the real roots of "Edison Village" had been pulled up and transplanted to New York City.

For a while Edison found himself totally involved in business matters, with little time left for inventing. His Pearl Street power station lost money at first and other cities didn't rush to order such stations.

There was a good reason for this. It cost a lot of money to set up a power station and wire an area for electricity. Therefore, it took quite a while for the system to make enough profit to pay for itself. Eventually, it would pay a great deal. But in the meantime, Edison—and his backers— must have had many anxious moments.

At the same time, though, they received a pleasant surprise. The demand for central power stations might not yet be great. But many businesses wanted "isolated" lighting plants—rather like what Edison had done for the S.S. *Columbia.*

Hotels, factories, theaters, and department stores all placed their orders. J.P. Morgan even ordered a lighting plant for his home. (He had a pit dug in his garden for the boiler and steam engine.) Eventually Edison had to set up another new company, the Edison Company for Isolated Lighting.

By this time, of course, Thomas Alva Edison was an American national hero. All sorts of people flocked to his door to meet the great man. A famous Hungarian violinist even played for him all through one night. But one group of people gave Edison fits—newspaper reporters. They kept smoking his cigars.

Finally he decided to get even with them. He bought a box of trick cigars. They looked like the real thing, but they were made of hair and paper. Edison put them in his desk and waited to see what would happen.

A couple of months later, the man who had sold him the fakes asked how they had worked. Edison looked blank. Then he began to rummage through his desk. He had forgotten all about the trick cigars.

And then the awful truth dawned on him. He must have smoked them all himself!

Edison's forgetful ways weren't so funny when it came to his family. Sometimes he forgot about them for weeks. When he did go home, he would flop down on a clean bed in his greasy clothes and promptly fall asleep.

He didn't seem to like his two sons, Tom Junior and Willie, very much. They simply weren't enough like him. Neither one showed much interest in mechanical things. Tom Junior wasn't any good at sports either.

A man as smart as Edison should have been able to figure out that sons aren't always carbon copies of their father. But that never seemed to occur to him. He didn't even give the boys a good education, although he certainly could have afforded to. But *he* hadn't had a good education and hadn't needed one. His sons could just be like him or else.

For some reason, he got along better with his daughter, Marion. When Marion was about ten, he gave her a pony and cart. When the family moved to New York, he sent her to a private school for girls. She was also the only child allowed to visit him at work.

Mary, Edison's wife, must have been very lonely at times. She was definitely afraid of burglars. One night when Edison got home late and crawled through a window, she almost shot him with the revolver she kept under her pillow.

Mary rarely complained about her life. Instead, she tried to keep busy with her friends and her children. After a while, she became popular as the wife of a famous man. By then Edison was able to buy her a few nice things, too.

In the last part of 1883, Edison again became ill—no doubt from overwork. So he, Mary, and Marion went to Saint Augustine, Florida, for a few weeks. He came back to New

York feeling fine. A Florida vacation every winter, he decided, might not be a bad idea.

The next summer, Mary and the children went back to Menlo Park, as they usually did for the warm months. In July, Mary came down with typhoid fever. At first it did not seem to be a serious case. But as time passed, she grew worse.

At last someone sent for Edison. He hurried out to Menlo Park. Then, on the morning of August 9, 1884, he waked Marion. He was crying so hard that he could barely speak. Finally he got the words out. Mary had died during the night. She wasn't even thirty years old.

After that, Edison wanted nothing more to do with Menlo Park. He let both the famous laboratory and the house fall into ruins. It was almost as if he felt *they* had taken his Mary away from him. Or maybe they reminded him of all the hours he could have spent with her, but didn't.

Some people said that Edison changed after Mary's death. He didn't seem as excited or energetic. He didn't dream such big dreams. It is true that all his major inventions came while she was still alive.

He tried to ease the pain of her death by throwing himself into his work again. He began to study something that he called "the Edison effect." He had noticed in light bulbs that some sort of particles seemed to be carried by an electrical force—without any wires and in a vacuum. He could tell this by the dark film they left on the inside of the glass bulbs. He even managed to use this discovery to make a better bulb. It was known as the Edison-effect lamp.

But after a while, he grew tired of this work. He never enjoyed experimenting with things he couldn't get his hands on. And what he actually had been observing in the bulbs was the movement of electrons, tiny particles of atoms.

If Edison had stayed with this research, he might have become a pioneer in the field of electronics as well as in electricity. Instead, Edison went back to his first love, the telegraph. He wanted to figure out a way to send and receive telegraph messages on a moving train. The instrument he invented became known as the "space" or "grasshopper" telegraph.

He also found a way to send telegraph messages up to three miles without using any wires. This system, he thought, could be used by ships to keep from colliding during foggy weather.

Meanwhile, politics in his various companies were constantly distracting him. The directors would not spend money. They wouldn't approve the promotion necessary to sell electric light systems to cities and towns. All they seemed to do was sit around and complain that profits weren't coming in fast enough.

The worst one of all, thought Edison, was Sherburne B. Eaton, president of Edison Electric Light. Fortunately,

Edison's good friend, Edward Johnson, was also on the board of directors. So Edison and Samuel Insull got Eaton kicked downstairs to the position of corporation counsel. A very old man, Eugene Crowell, was chosen to be president. All the power now rested in the hands of the executive vice-president, Edward Johnson.

At once Johnson began filing lawsuits against people who were stealing Edison's ideas. More important, he had the Pearl Street power station enlarged and began work on two new stations in other parts of the city. Suddenly business boomed and Edison was able to sit back and heave a sigh of relief.

He had renewed an old friendship with a man from Cincinnati, Ezra Gilliland, who worked in the Edison laboratory. Gilliland and his wife tried to get the young widower out into society a little more. Mary had been dead for six months. The boys were staying with their Aunt Alice. Marion was at boarding school in New York. And Edison was lonely.

He liked the Gillilands and their friends. He went so far as to buy some new clothes to look presentable when he was with them. Together they sailed in yachts, listened to music, and chitchatted about what they had written in their diaries. This was a contrast to the Edison who usually stomped around his factories in old boots and smoked nickel cigars!

Of course Mrs. Gilliland knew exactly what Edison

needed—another wife. She invited lovely young girls to visit when Edison was around. One of them came all the way from Akron, Ohio. Her name was Mina Miller and she was beautiful.

But it wasn't her beauty that most impressed Edison, or the way she played the piano and sang. Miss Mina Miller didn't seem to be afraid of him! When he stared at her, she stared right back.

That made her unforgettable to Edison and, as time went on, she seemed to drift more and more into his thoughts. In the winter of 1885, he caught a bad cold and almost died from complications. When he was able to travel, Mrs. Gilliland and Marion whisked him off to Florida for a long vacation. His thoughts of Mina went along. And followed him back to New York.

"Saw a lady who looked like Mina," he wrote. "Got thinking about Mina and came near being run over by a streetcar. If Mina interferes much more will have to take out an accident policy."

There was only one solution to this problem. He must marry Mina. And, while he was at it, he would build a winter home for them in Florida. A laboratory there, too. And a house for the Gillilands.

Now, all he had to do was to get Mina to say yes.

For a while, he had to do his wooing by mail—all the way to Ohio. When Mina and her family came to spend the summer in Jamestown, New York, Edison rushed up to visit them.

Unfortunately, though, he couldn't seem to get much time alone with Mina. There were always all those *people* around. So many extra voices and eager ears didn't help a whispering lover who couldn't hear very well in the first place.

Edison came up with a solution to that problem, too. He taught Mina Morse code. Then the two of them tapped messages on each other's hands and no one else had the faintest notion of what was going on.

One afternoon during a carriage ride, he tapped out a message asking Mina to marry him.

"Yes," she tapped back. But she wanted her parents' approval.

They gave it.

After that, Edison shifted into high gear. One moment he was working on all the new buildings in Florida. The next he was looking for another home near New York. Twice he went to Akron to visit Mina and once she came to New York.

During that visit, he showed her the home he had found in West Orange, New Jersey. Its name was Glenmont. Mina must have been amazed the first time she saw it.

Glenmont was a castle, complete with outbuildings, greenhouses, balconies, stained-glass windows, and fancy gardens. Statues stood around everywhere and the walls were covered with oil paintings.

On February 24, 1886, the two were married at Mina's family home in Akron. It was not a quiet ceremony. Horse-drawn carriages drove back and forth between the house and the train station, carrying guests from everywhere. Flowers filled the rooms and an orchestra played. The luncheon waiters were imported from Chicago.

After lunch, the newlyweds drove around Akron, smiling and accepting the cheers of local citizens. Then, in the evening, they climbed aboard a train and set off for a long honeymoon in Florida.

Edison dictating his morning's correspondence into his phonograph

## Chapter 11

# LIGHTS OUT FOR EDISON

In his middle years, Edison found himself part of the business boom that was exploding all over the United States. He moved his machine works to Schenectady, New York, where there was room to spread out. He built a huge laboratory in West Orange, New Jersey. As far as he was concerned—and as far as everyone else was concerned—bigger was better.

But then an event drove Edison back to his drawing table. Chichester Bell (a cousin of Alexander Graham Bell) and Charles Tainter began to work on the phonograph.

Edison was furious. How *dare* they do such a thing? The phonograph was his—all his.

He didn't seem to remember that *he* had worked on someone else's telephone. He wouldn't admit that he had ignored the phonograph for ten years. It was *his* baby, he told everyone, and he had been thinking about it all along.

It was time to turn thoughts to actions. Edison got busy. When Bell and Tainter suggested they work together, he told them to get lost. He would do the work on his own. Furthermore, he added, he would ruin them.

For two years Edison experimented with improvements on his "baby." He was convinced that the phonograph would be used most by business people to dictate letters. He invented wax cylinders to take the place of the old tinfoil sheets. He figured out a way to scrape off layers of wax so the cylinders could be used over and over. He improved devices for recording and for playing.

Edison's lab notes list some of the problems to be solved if his phonograph were to be a practical machine:

> Crackling sounds in addition to continuous scraping due, either to blow-holes, or particles of wax not brushed off—poor recording— uneven tracking—dulling of the recorder point— breaking of glass diaphram—knocking sound: chips in wax cylinder—humming sound, due to motor.

Meanwhile, in April of 1888, Bell and Tainter sold the patent to their phonograph (which they called a graphophone) to a man named Jesse Lippincott. He was going to sell the machine for them.

Work harder! Work faster! Edison urged his men.

June came and he was almost ready to release his machine. Then he changed his mind. It wasn't *quite* good enough.

All right, he said. The crew would work day and night until it *was* good enough. No one would be allowed to see them—not reporters, not even their families. Edison himself had a new baby daughter when he gave that order. Madeleine had been born in May. But work came first.

Reporters said the "great vigil" lasted five days. According to the lab books, it lasted seventy-two hours. At any rate, on June 16, 1888, Edison sent a record (called a "phonogram") to his friend George Gouraud in England.

When Gouraud played it, he heard Edison's voice saying:

> In my Laboratory in Orange, N.J.
> June 16, 1888 3 o'clock A. M.
>
> Friend Gouraud:
>
> This is my first mailing phonogram. It will go to you in the regular U.S. mail via North German Lloyd steamer *Eider*. I send you by Mr. Hamilton a new phonograph, the first one of the new model which has just left my hands.
>
> It has been put together very hurriedly and is not finished, as you will see. I have sent you a quantity of experimental phonogram blanks, and music by every mail leaving here. . . .
>
> Mrs. Edison and the baby are doing well. The baby's articulation is quite loud enough but a trifle indistinct; it can be improved but it is not bad for a first experiment.
>
> With kind regards,
>
> Yours, EDISON

Gouraud demonstrated the phonograph in England. Once again Edison was a hero there. But a famous composer, Sir Arthur Sullivan, was a little worried. He said (on a record):

I am astonished and somewhat terrified at the results of this evening's experiments. Astonished at the wonderful power you have developed, and terrified at the thought that so much hideous and bad music may be put on record forever.

Said Edison, "I don't want the phonograph sold for amusement purposes. It is not a toy. I want it sold for business purposes only."

For once he did a terrible job of predicting the future!

Unfortunately he didn't do a very good job of picking some friends either. As his business interests grew more complicated, he gave more and more power to two men, Ezra Gilliland and a young lawyer, John Tomlinson.

Of course he had every reason to trust Gilliland. He had known the man for years. After Mary died, the Gillilands had helped him put his life back together. They had even introduced him to Mina. So when the time came to sell his patent rights on the phonograph, he put Gilliland and Tomlinson in charge of the deal.

The man who wanted to buy the rights was Jesse Lippincott—the same man who owned Bell and Tainter's rights.

That didn't bother Edison. He was used to fighting with a financial wizard one minute and taking his money the next.

What did bother him, though, was Lippincott's offer. Edison had been hoping for a million dollars. According to Gilliland and Tomlinson, Lippincott would give only half a million.

Take it, they urged the inventor. It's the best offer you'll get.

So Edison took it. The day after the deal was completed, Gilliland and Tomlinson and their families left for Europe. The two men were supposed to sell patent rights for the phonograph there, too. Just before they left, Edison gave Tomlinson seven thousand dollars to help pay for the trip.

He never saw Gilliland or Tomlinson again.

It was Lippincott who finally caught on to what had happened. He told Edison about all the "secret bargains" the two men had made with him. Those "secret bargains" cheated Edison out of hundreds of thousands of dollars.

He never got the money back. Since Gilliland and Tomlinson had legal power to act for Edison, what they did was not fraud. It was "only a breach of ethics."

I'll never trust anyone again, said Edison. And, with one exception, he meant it.

Mina Edison must have been very hurt, too. After all, Mrs. Gilliland had been one of her closest friends. But she did everything she could to cheer up her husband. He was tired, she realized, as well as sad. What he needed was a long rest. How about a trip to Europe? They sailed to France in August of 1889.

Paris welcomed Edison with open arms. Government officials and crowds of people swarmed around wherever he went. The president of France made him a commander of the French Legion of Honor. Banquet followed banquet.

Edison didn't much like the banquets. His favorite meal took place high on the Eiffel Tower. There he had lunch with the designer of the tower, Alexandre Gustave Eiffel.

He also met some famous scientists. In Paris he visited Louis Pasteur, the man who saved millions of lives through his work with diseases such as tuberculosis and rabies. In Germany he met Hermann von Helmholtz, a great physicist, and Werner von Siemens, who worked with electricity.

In England, S.Z. Ferranti also worked with electricity. But his ideas were quite different from Edison's. Edison had always used direct current (d.c.). Ferranti was experimenting with alternating current (a.c.). Alternating current was much more powerful and could go much farther.

Too powerful and too dangerous, thought Edison. As far as he was concerned, alternating current would never work.

When he and Mina returned from Europe, feeling great, Edison found a fresh batch of headaches waiting for him.

Early in 1889, many of his companies had been merged to form Edison General Electric. Now Edison G.E. found itself with some serious competitors. One was Thomson-Houston

Electric, that tiny company that had seemed so harmless a few years back. Another was a company headed by George Westinghouse. Both Thomson-Houston and Westinghouse worked with alternating current.

They were going to kill people that way! raged Edison. Direct current was the only safe method. Couldn't they *see* that?

Westinghouse disagreed. Alternating current was perfectly safe, he insisted.

And so the "battle of the currents" began.

Edison *was* wrong. Soon everyone, including the directors of Edison General Electric, realized this. But stubbornly he stuck to his guns.

In 1892, Edison won an important lawsuit against Westinghouse. But it was a costly victory and more expensive court battles loomed ahead. If the electric companies went on fighting one another, they all would go broke. Besides, the patent on the electric lamp was to run out in just two more years. Then anybody could make one.

There seemed to be just one answer to the problem: another merger.

On April 15, 1892, that is what took place. Thomson-Houston and Edison General Electric merged. The new company was called the General Electric Company.

Edison was hurt and angry—especially because his name had been dropped. But he also felt relieved. He was tired of

working with electricity and of all the business entangle-
ments that went with it. He wouldn't really mind walking
away from the whole thing.

Besides, he had some new projects in mind. Maybe he
would go underground for a while. . . .

## Chapter 12

# FLOPS AND MARVELS

Go underground Edison did—literally. He headed up to northwestern New Jersey and began digging. A huge steam shovel and a giant crane towered against the sky like prehistoric beasts. Other machines crunched up rocks and spit them out again. Mountains were chewed and blasted away.

Through all the noise and dust wandered Edison, happy as a child with a new game to play.

What is the man up to? people wondered. Is he searching for gold?

Not exactly. But he was trying to find valuable metal. Industries were demanding more and more iron. In many places rich iron ore had already been mined out. What remained was a less valuable, less rich resource called "lean ore." With the right equipment, thought Edison, he could get plenty of iron from "lean ore."

He, of course, would invent the equipment.

So he leased or bought nineteen thousand acres of land near Ogdensburg, New Jersey, obtained some machinery, hired some men, and dug in. He had the money to do what he wanted. He had made a small fortune on the electric company mergers. And he loved the work.

Once again his family took a backseat as he devoted himself to the "Ogden Baby." Mina gave birth to two babies while he was busy mining. They were named Charles and Theodore. Tom Junior got into financial problems. Will caught scarlet fever. Sam Edison, his father, died.

But none of these events seemed as important to Edison as his rocks and machines. He invented a magnetic separator, a rock-crushing machine, and better conveyor belts. He figured out new ways to make iron-ore briquettes.

Still, the project was doomed to fail. Other sources of rich iron ore were discovered. Iron ore prices kept dropping.

"We might as well blow the whistle and close up shop." Edison finally admitted.

His "Ogden Baby" had cost five years of his life and several million dollars.

"Well, it's all gone," he said with a smile. "But we had ... a good time spending it!"

During those five years, he had had some other good times, too. One summer he worked with a young writer, George Parsons Lathrop, on the plot of a science-fiction novel. Edison dreamed up the ideas and Lathrop put them in story form.

Artificial diamonds in daily use. New plastic materials. Food made by chemists. Heavier-than-air flying machines. Trips to Mars. Wars "conducted by dropping dynamite from balloons."

Those were just some of Edison's ideas. After a while, he lost interest in the project and went back to his rocks.

During another break, he became interested in an early X-ray machine, called a fluoroscope. The discoverer of the rays and what they could do was a man in Germany, W.K. Roentgen. Then many inventors set to work to make machines that would use the rays in practical ways.

One problem was finding the right chemicals for the fluoroscope. A professor at Columbia University, Michael Pupin, asked Edison to do some research. Edison and his staff experimented with some eight thousand combinations before they came up with one they liked.

Edison sent a fluoroscope using this combination to Pupin. Pupin then X-rayed a man's hand that was filled with shotgun pellets. A surgeon used the X-ray as a guide while he removed the pellets. It was the first X-ray surgery ever performed in the United States.

Edison stopped working with fluoroscopes, though, when scientists began to realize how dangerous X-rays could be. Instead he turned back to his rocks and to his "secret invention."

That "secret invention" had been important to him for a number of years. As soon as he returned from Europe in October of 1889, he rushed to his laboratory in West Orange to see how it was coming along. One of his assistants, W.K.L. Dickson, took him into a large, dark room and asked him to sit down in front of a screen. Then Dickson went to the back of the room and began to fiddle with a machine.

Suddenly Edison saw a picture of Dickson moving on the screen. The picture-Dickson tipped its hat and smiled.

"Good morning, Mr. Edison," it said. "Glad to see you back. I hope you are satisfied with the Kineto-phonograph."

Later, the Kineto-phonograph would be known as a motion picture camera. Edison couldn't see any practical use for it. But it fascinated him anyway.

He had begun by taking a series of tiny pictures directly on a plaster cylinder. Then, in 1889, John Carbutt invented celluloid film and another inventor, George Eastman, improved it. Celluloid film worked much better than the plaster cylinder. Edison put holes in the side of the film and invented a machine with a sproket wheel that would feed and rewind the film automatically. Then he invented a little peephole box in which people could see the moving pictures. This he called a kinetoscope.

During the summer of 1891, newspapers began to print articles about these exciting new inventions. Time to file for patents, thought Edison. But he did a sloppy job of it that caused him trouble later. He simply didn't realize what a marvel he had created.

In 1893 he wrote to a friend:

I have constructed a little instrument which

I call a Kinetoscope, with a nickel and slot attachment. Some 25 have been made, but am very doubtful if there is any commercial feature in it, and fear they will not even earn their cost. These . . . devices are of too sentimental a character to get the public to invest in."

Even so, Edison went ahead and built a motion-picture studio at West Orange. It looked like a big shed, mounted on a pivot so it could be turned to follow the sun. Half the roof opened on hinges to let the sun in.

The films were each about a minute long. They showed boxing matches, dancing girls, acrobats, animals, and even some poor person in a dentist's chair.

Edison's usual money men didn't think there was much future for moving pictures either. But two other men, Norman Raff and Frank Gammon, felt differently. In 1894 they formed a business called the Kinetoscope Company. They bought a large number of Edison's peephole machines and began opening "kinetoscope parlors" in major cities across the country.

People loved them. They stood in line for hours just to see one tiny film of boxers fighting. When Edison supplied a six-reel show of an especially important fight, police had to be called in to handle the huge crowd of eager viewers at the New York parlor.

To watch a six-reel film, people had to move to six different kinetoscopes. That was a bit awkward. A picture projected on one big screen would certainly work better. But so far, the means of doing so hadn't been perfected.

For a while Edison worked on the problem. Then he gave it up. If he made a machine that could project good pictures on a screen, he said, he would be able to sell only about ten of them. He was quite sure there never would be more than ten movie theaters in the United States.

So other inventors got into the act. Men in France, England, and the United States all came up with advances. At last Edison had to admit that he was wrong—and in a very painful way. He had to let his name be put on a film projector invented by another man, Thomas Armat. He didn't claim to be the inventor of Armat's machine. But he let his name help sell it.

Eventually, though, Edison's motion-picture companies did well. In fact, they helped him recover from the financially disasterous "Ogden Baby." Then, with both rocks and movies out of the way, Edison turned to yet another new idea. (He sometimes told people that he had enough ideas to break the Bank of England.)

This new idea had to do with the horseless carriage. Edison was certain that the automobile of the future would have an electric motor powered by a storage battery. He wanted to work on the storage battery.

Oddly enough, he had met a thin young man named Henry Ford a few years earlier. At that time, Ford worked in a Detroit Edison company. But he also had an idea for an automobile—one that would run on gasoline.

"Young man, that's the thing! You have it!" Edison said when Ford told him his idea.

The famous inventor's approval was great encouragement for Ford. Soon he set up his own company to make automobiles. It was just a small company then, but—

Meanwhile, though, Edison was working to perfect a storage battery for electric cars. During that period, around 1900, batteries had to be tremendously heavy to give much power. Edison's plan was to invent a lighter, more economical battery.

Once again he began thousands of experiments. By this time, of course, he had an army of scientists in his laboratory to help him. But progress was slow.

When a friend said he was sorry how badly things were going, Edison replied, "Why, man, I've got a lot of results. I know several thousand things that won't work."

He had unusual methods of quality control, too. To test the hardness of his batteries, he had workmen throw them out of the second- and third-story windows of the laboratory!

At last, in the summer of 1904, he was ready to start manufacturing.

"It's here! The newest Edison marvel!" cried the newspapers. People gobbled up the batteries. Edison was flying high. He said:

> Yes, the new battery will settle the horse—not at once but by degrees. The price of automobiles will be reduced. . . . In fact, I hope that the time has nearly arrived when every man may not only be able to light his own house, but charge his own machinery, heat his rooms, cook his food, etc., by electricity, without depending on anyone else for these services.

Then came the bad news. Many of the batteries didn't work. They leaked and they lost power. Edison didn't hesitate. He took back all the bad batteries, returned the customers' money, shut down his factory, and went back to experimenting.

It took five more years of very hard work. But in 1909, Edison could write to one of his customers, "At last the battery is finished."

Much to his disappointment, though, his battery never was used much in automobiles. That skinny young man, Henry Ford, had a better idea with his gasoline-powered cars. But people did find plenty of other uses for the Edison battery. It was used in miners' lamps, train lights, and sea machinery. It worked well for quarrying, railroad signaling, and radio telegraphy. Power stations kept Edison batteries on hand in case of emergencies and the military used them to run submarines.

Edison didn't make a lot of money from his storage battery—although he made some. But money was never important to him—at least not money for its own sake. Henry Ford once called him "the world's greatest inventor and worst businessman." Edison might have agreed.

"I always invent," he said, "to obtain money to go on inventing."

And he *did* end up a multimillionaire.

Punching a time clock

Chapter 13

# "THE OLD MAN"

"The Old Man." That's what Edison's co-workers at the lab called him now. But they spoke the words with their own tough kind of respect.

"Secrets have to be long-winded and roost high to get away when the Old Man goes hunting for them," said one of those co-workers.

Cement held a few secrets that Edison was now hunting. He wanted to build better machinery and a better kiln for making cement. He did it.

Why not construct some of his own factory buildings from poured cement? He did that, too.

How about poured-cement houses for his workers? That didn't work so well—yet.

Edison wasn't finished with the secrets of the phonograph either. Many of his competitors now were using wax discs instead of cylinders and he finally decided to join them. But he also invented a better disc—and a diamond needle—and an inexpensive player that almost anyone could afford.

There were still some bad times, such as the terrible fire in 1914 that gutted most of his factories in West Orange. Edison lost almost a million dollars in the blaze. But, as he said to someone who offered him sympathy, "I am sixty-seven, but I'm not too old to make a fresh start."

Henry Ford lent him $750,000 toward that fresh start. In about a month, Edison had the factories humming again. (He paid Ford back, too.)

When World War I began, Edison at first wanted the United States to have nothing to do with it. Later, though, he changed his mind. He even headed a board of inventors and scientists that advised the military. He talked the navy into setting up its own research laboratory—although not until after the war—and he worked on defense equipment to use against German U-boats.

Some of Edison's bad times came about because of his children. He had not been a good father to Tom Junior and Will. That caused problems in later years.

For a while, Tom Junior drank too much and got involved with some shady characters. At one point, Edison had to disown him—for legal reasons. Finally, though, the two became friends again and Tom worked in his father's companies.

Will liked to spend money and have a good time. He also loved adventure. He fought in the Spanish-American War and in World War I. But he refused to have anything to do with Mina, his stepmother, so he grew away from his family.

Marion, her father's favorite, was also jealous of Mina at first, but she got over it. For a number of years she lived in

Europe. When she came home again, she was close to her whole family—including her half brothers and half sister.

Those three—Mina's children—enjoyed a very different life from the first three. Mina insisted that Edison spend at least a *little* time with them. She also made sure they got good educations and a chance to do what they wanted with their lives.

Madeleine, the first child, attended Bryn Mawr College. Then she became Mrs. John Sloane and lived in New Jersey.

Charles, the older son, went to Massachusetts Institute of Technology. He liked to write, but his real goal was to go into his father's business—and he did. After Edison retired, Charles became head of Thomas A. Edison, Inc.

The younger son, Theodore, went to M.I.T., also. But he wanted to be a mathematical physicist. Edison couldn't believe it. A son of *his* good at math? Still, he got used to the idea and even built a laboratory for Theodore.

It was Charles and Theodore who told their father he should be working on electronic phonographs and radio receivers. "The Old Man" was in his late seventies by then and hated the idea. His mechanical phonograph was better, he said. As for the radio—why, it was a craze that would never last.

For a while Charles and Theodore worked on the electronic phonograph in secret. Then Edison found out what they were doing. Did he erupt in anger? Did he order them to stop? No, he decided to work on one himself and beat them at their own game!

Finally the Edison company did put out an electronic phonograph and began making radio receivers, too. But Edison had waited too long and neither project succeeded very well.

Meanwhile, Edison had found a new way to have a good time. He began going on automobile trips with his friends Henry Ford, Harvey Firestone (the tire manufacturer), and John Burroughs (the naturalist).

It all began with a trip by Burroughs, Edison, and Ford to the Florida Everglades. Burroughs gave the inventors lessons in nature. Ford and Edison were eager students.

Later, Ford took Edison and Firestone to the California plantation of Luther Burbank, a great botanist. Edison was entranced. Botany! Why, he'd never done anything with plants—except for that work with bamboo.

Then, in the summer of 1916, came the first auto trip. Edison, Firestone, and Burroughs set out for ten days "back to nature" in New England and New York State. True, they had servants and drivers with them. But bouncing along back roads in early automobiles was no picnic. Besides, they did live in tents, sleep in their clothes, wash in creeks, and cook over camp fires.

Ford joined them for the next trip two years later. This time they went all the way to the Smoky Mountains. Unfortunately, a group of reporters joined them too, their pens scratching away and their cameras clicking. That made Edison angry, but it didn't stop him from having a marvelous time.

He usually did have a good time when he was with Henry Ford. By now the two men were excellent friends. Ford almost worshiped Edison—the man who had encouraged him when he was just beginning. As far as Edison was concerned, Ford was the only man he ever really trusted after Gilliland and Tomlinson's betrayal.

"As to Henry Ford," he once said, "words are inadequate to express my feelings. I can only say to you, that in the fullest and richest meaning of the terms—he is my best friend."

He said those words in a speech given at the "Golden Jubilee of Light." This great festival was put on by Ford and General Electric in October of 1929. It was a giant party celebrating the fiftieth birthday of Edison's electric lamp.

The jubilee took place on Ford's property in Dearborn, Michigan. Many important people attended, including President and Mrs. Herbert Hoover, Marie Curie (the famous physicist), Orville Wright (the airplane pioneer), and, of course, a whole flock of financial wizards.

Ford gave the best present—to Edison and to the American people. He had built a little town, called Greenfield Village, a museum of American history and inventions.

Needless to say, much of Greenfield Village was—and is—about Edison's life and work. Ford had rebuilt there the Menlo Park laboratory (along with Mrs. Jordan's boarding-house), the Pearl Street power station, and a train station in Michigan where Edison had worked as a boy. He even arranged for a reproduction of a Grand Trunk Railway train, complete with Edison's portable laboratory in the baggage car.

When Ford asked him what he thought of all this, Edison replied, "You've got this just about ninety-nine and one-half percent perfect."

"What is the matter with the other one-half percent?" Ford wanted to know.

"Well," said Edison, "we never kept it as clean as this!"

By then Edison was in his eighties. He had retired officially from his companies. That didn't mean he had stopped working. He remembered how excited he'd been about botany while at Luther Burbank's plantation. And—being Edison—he got busy.

Ford and Firestone suggested the project: find a plant that could be used to make rubber quickly and that would grow in the United States. At that time, all rubber came from plants growing in tropical areas. This could be a real problem for the United States in case a war were to cut off rubber supplies.

Edison did most of his plant research in his Florida home.

But he followed the same old procedure: read all he could, then experiment and experiment some more. He tested around fourteen thousand plants before de decided the best bet grew wild over much of the United States—goldenrod.

Next he crossbred different kinds of goldenrod to get a strain that would give a lot of latex (from which rubber is made). He ended up with a goldenrod plant fourteen feet tall (guaranteed to scare to death anyone with hay fever!).

Processing the goldenrod latex was his next problem. Here he ran into real trouble. He simply couldn't get the rubber made cheaply enough to be practical. He *knew* he could make his idea work if he just had enough time.

Time, though, was something he didn't have. Even if he had, goldenrod rubber would have disappointed him in the end. Synthetic rubber made from coal or petroleum was the answer. Other scientists already were beginning to suspect that.

But Edison now was having trouble with his health. He suffered a serious illness in the summer of 1929 and another that fall. Doctors found at least four things wrong with him—an ulcer, diabetes, Bright's disease, and uremic poisoning. They couldn't understand how he went on functioning.

He didn't go to the laboratory very often during his last two years. But he kept tabs on what was happening there and went for automobile rides with Mina almost every day.

Edison in front of his ore mining plant in 1895

Once they drove to the Newark airport. Edison was very interested in planes and wanted to learn more about them. He was also interested in atomic energy.

"There will one day spring from the brain of Science," he said, "a machine or force so fearful in its potentialities, so absolutely terrifying, that even man . . . will be appalled and so will abandon war forever. . . ."

In August of 1931, Edison became so weak that his doctors thought he would die. He didn't, but from then on spent most of his time in his bedroom. By October, he was slipping in and out of comas. He spoke his last words as he sat by his bedroom window, looking out at the lawn and trees.

"It is very beautiful over there," he said.

Early in the morning of Sunday, October 18, 1931, Thomas Alva Edison died. His funeral took place on Wednesday, October 21. That day people all across the United States paid their final tribute to the inventor who had given them so much.

For just a few moments, they dimmed their lights.

# Thomas Alva Edison 1847-1931

1847 Thomas Alva Edison is born in Vienna, Ontario.

1848 Zachary Taylor is elected U.S. president. Gold is discovered in California; the gold rush begins. Thomas Kelvin devises a scale of absolute temperatures. Chewing gum and air conditioning first appear in U.S.

1849 Joseph Henry receives first telegraphed weather report. French physicist Armand Fizeau measures the speed of light. George Corliss patents a four-valved steam engine.

1850 Millard Fillmore becomes U.S. president, following Zachary Taylor's death. Congress passes Compromise of 1850, designating states as slave or free. John Brett sends a telegraph message across the English Channel via underwater cable.

1851 The U.S. coins three-cent pieces, and sets the postage rate at three cents for a half-ounce letter. *New York Times* is founded. Inventor Isaac Singer patents the sewing machine.

1852 Franklin Pierce is elected president. Harriet Beecher Stowe publishes *Uncle Tom's Cabin*.

1854 Kansas-Nebraska Act is passed; U.S. territories now choose whether or not to have slavery; Republican party is formed as a reaction to this act.

1855 Bitter war rages between pro- and anti-slavery factions in Kansas. David Hughes invents a printing telegraph.

1856 James Buchanan is elected president. Western Union telegraph company is established. Henry Bessemer invents a process for converting iron to steel.

1857 Supreme Court issues the pro-slavery Dred Scott Decision.

1858 Abraham Lincoln and Stephen Douglas debate slavery issue. First transatlantic telegraph cable is completed; British Queen Victoria and U.S. President Buchanan exchange messages.

1859 Abolitionist John Brown leads a raid on Harper's Ferry, West Virginia; he is captured and hanged. Moses Farmer develops a briefly-burning incandescent lamp.

1860 Abraham Lincoln is elected president. South Carolina secedes from the Union.

1861 Ten southern states secede from the Union, forming the Confederate States of America and electing Jefferson Davis president; Confederate attack on Fort Sumter begins Civil War.

1862 Robert E. Lee heads Confederate army; Civil War battles fought at Antietam, Fredericksburg, and Chattanooga; *Monitor* and *Merrimac* engage in first ironclad sea battle.

1863 Emancipation Proclamation: Abraham Lincoln declares all slaves free. Lincoln delivers Gettysburg address.

1864 Abraham Lincoln is reelected president. Ulysses S. Grant commands Union army. Union General William Sherman begins march through Georgia; Savannah, Georgia, surrenders to Union army. George Pullman invents first railroad sleeping car.

1865 Confederate General Robert E. Lee surrenders to Union General Ulysses S. Grant at Appomattox Court House, Virginia; Civil War ends. President Abraham Lincoln is assassinated; Andrew Johnson succeeds him. Thirteenth Amendment abolishes slavery. First international telegraph congress is held in Paris.

1866 Transatlantic telegraph cable is completed. Robert Whitehead invents the torpedo.

1867 U.S. buys Alaska from Russia for $7,200,000. Swedish chemist Alfred Nobel invents dynamite. Reconstruction Acts are passed.

1868 President Andrew Johnson is impeached, but later acquitted. Ulysses S. Grant is elected president. Edison patents his first invention, an electric vote counter.

1869  Edison invents the Edison Universal Stock Printer. First U.S. transcontinental railroad is completed. Russian chemist Dmitri Mendeleev organizes chemical elements into the periodic table.

1871  Edison marries Mary Stillwell in Newark, New Jersey. Chicago is devastated by the Great Chicago Fire.

1872  Ulysses S. Grant is reelected U.S. president. Englishman Edwaerd Muybridge, an early experimenter in motion pictures, photographs a horse in motion.

1874  Edison invents the quadruplex telegraph, which can send four messages at once over one wire.

1875  Richard Hoe invents the rotary printing press.

1876  Edison sets up a laboratory in Menlo Park, New Jersey. Alexander Graham Bell patents the telephone. Rutherford B. Hayes is elected president. Sitting Bull massacres General Custer's troops at Little Big Horn. Centennial Exhibition in Philadelphia features the electric arc light, or gaslight. Mark Twain publishes *The Adventures of Tom Sawyer*.

1877  Edison invents the phonograph.

1878  Sir Joseph Swan invents a type of incandescent electric lamp. David Hughes invents the microphone.

1879  Edison invents the incandescent electric lamp, with a circuit to keep several lamps burning at once. William Crookes invents the cathode ray tube.

1881  James Garfield is assassinated; Chester A. Arthur becomes president.

1882  Edison designs the first hydroelectric plant, in Appleton, Wisconsin. New York City installs first electric street lamps. U.S. bans Chinese immigration for next ten years.

1883  Northern Pacific Railroad line is completed. World's first skyscraper, 10 stories high, is built in Chicago. New York's Brooklyn Bridge is opened. Robert Koch develops an anthrax vaccine. "Buffalo Bill" Cody opens his Wild West Show. Robert Louis Stevenson publishes *Treasure Island*.

1884  Edison's first wife, Mary, dies. Grover Cleveland is elected president. First intercity telephone lines go into use, between Boston and New York City. France presents the Statue of Liberty to the U.S. World's first subway opens in London. Mark Twain publishes *The Adventures of Huckleberry Finn*.

1885  Civil War General Ulysses S. Grant dies. Chichester Bell and Charles Tainter patent a phonograph that uses a wax cylinder. Karl Auer von Welsbach invents the incandescent gas mantle. Louis Pasteur develops a rabies vaccine. George Eastman invents coated photographic paper. William Burroughs invents the adding machine. John M. Fox introduces golf to the U.S.

1886  Edison marries Mina Miller. Anarchists riot in Chicago's Haymarket Square. German chemist Clemens Winkler discovers the element germanium. Coca-Cola first goes on sale. Robert Louis Stevenson publishes *Doctor Jekyll and Mr. Hyde*.

1887  Edison builds the Edison Laboratory in West Orange, N.J. Edison and J.W. Swan collaborate to produce Ediswan electric lamps. German physicist Heinrich Hertz produces electromagnetic waves. Sir Arthur Conan Doyle publishes first Sherlock Holmes mystery.

1888  Benjamin Harrison is elected president. Nikola Tesla invents an electric motor using alternating current. Karl Benz of Germany invents the first gasoline-powered automobile. George Eastman invents the Kodak box camera.

1891  Edison patents the kinetoscope, a motion picture camera. Dutch anthropologist Eugene Dubois discovers remains of the prehistoric Java Man. Whitcomb L. Judson invents the zipper.

1892  Grover Cleveland is elected president. First telephone switchboard is introduced. Diesel patents an internal combustion engine.

1893 World Columbian Exhibition opens in Chicago. Henry Ford constructs his first automobile.

1894 Edison opens "Kinetoscope Parlor" in New York.

1895 Guglielmo Marconi invents the wireless telegraph. Auguste and Louis Lumière invent a motion picture camera. Wilhelm von Roentgen discovers X-rays. King Gillette invents the safety razor.

1896 William McKinley is elected president. Klondike gold rush begins in Alaska. French physicist Henry Becquerel discovers radioactivity. First modern Olympic games are held. Cracker Jacks and Tootsie Rolls are introduced in the U.S..

1897 Scottish physicist Joseph Thomson discovers the electron. German physicist Karl Braun invents the oscilloscope. First U.S. subway line opens in Boston.

1898 Spanish-American war begins, and ends in Treaty of Paris; U.S. acquires the Philippines, Puerto Rico, and Guam. U.S. annexes Hawaii. Marie and Pierre Curie discover radium.

1899 Edison Illuminating Company and Consolidated Gas Company merge to form New York's Consolidated Edison Company.

1900 William McKinley is reelected president. German physicist Max Planck introduces the quantum theory. Ferdinand von Zepplin launches the first rigid airship.

1901 President William McKinley is assassinated; Theodore Roosevelt becomes president. Guglielmo Marconi sends first transatlantic radio signals. First Nobel prizes are awarded, from a fund given by Alfred Nobel, inventor of dynamite.

1903 Orville and Wilbur Wright fly the first airplane at Kitty Hawk, North Carolina.

1904 Theodore Roosevelt is elected president. Photographs are first transmitted telegraphically. J.P.L. Elster invents the photoelectric cell.

1905 Albert Einstein introduces his special theory of relativity. First neon light signs are used.

1906 First voice and music program is broadcast on radio.

1907 President Roosevelt bars Japanese immigration. Lee de Forest invents the triode vacuum tube. First electric washing machine is invented in Chicago.

1908 William Howard Taft is elected president. Ford Motor Company manufactures the first Model "T" car.

1909 Motion picture newsreels first appear in theaters.

1911 Tungsten filament is first used in electric light bulbs.

1912 Woodrow Wilson is elected president.

1913 Edison begins producing phonograph discs and a machine to play them.

1914 World War I begins.

1915 Germans sink *Lusitania*. Telegraph service opens between U.S. and Japan. Einstein introduces his general theory of relativity. Alexander Graham Bell in New York and Thomas Watson in San Francisco have the first transcontinental telephone conversation.

1916 Woodrow Wilson is reelected president.

1917 U.S. enters World War I. First jazz phonograph recordings are made.

1918 World War I ends. Airmail service and daylight saving time begin in U.S.

1920 Warren G. Harding is elected president. Nineteenth Amendment gives women the right to vote. First public radio broadcasting stations open in U.S. and England.

1923 President Warren Harding dies; Calvin Coolidge becomes president; Coolidge delivers first presidential radio address.

1924 Calvin Coolidge wins presidential election. J. Edgar Hoover becomes head of Bureau of Investigation (later called Federal Bureau of Investigation). RCA transmits photographs from New York to London by wireless telegraphy.

1925 Bell Laboratories is established for physics research.

1926 John Logie Baird gives first public demonstration of television. First transatlantic radiotelephone conversation takes place.

1927 Charles A. Lindberg makes first solo airplane flight across the Atlantic. Belgian George Lemaître introduces "big bang" theory of the origin of the universe. "The Jazz Singer" is the first motion picture with sound.

1928 Herbert Hoover is elected president. Congress approves $32 million to enforce Prohibition. Amelia Earhart is first woman to fly across the Atlantic. Walt Disney releases first Mickey Mouse films.

1929 U.S. stock market craches; Great Depression begins.

1930 More than 1300 U.S. banks close due to stock market crash.

1931 Edison dies on October 18. Wiley Post and Harold Gatty are the first to fly around the world. Ernest Lawrence invents the cyclotron, or "atom smasher."

# INDEX- *Page numbers in boldface type indicate illustrations.*

125

## ABOUT THE AUTHOR

Carol Greene has a B.A. in English Literature from Park College, Parkville, Missouri and an M.A. in Musicology from Indiana University, Bloomington. She's worked with international exchange programs, taught music and writing, and edited children's books. She now works as a free-lance writer in St. Louis, Missouri and has published over twenty books for children and a few for adults. When she isn't writing, Ms. Greene likes to read, travel, sing, and do volunteer work at her church. Some of her other books for Childrens Press include: *Louisa May Alcott: Author, Nurse, Suffragette; Marie Curie: Pioneer Physicist; Enchantment of the World: England; The Super Snoops and the Missing Sleepers; Sandra Day O'Conner: First Woman on the Supreme Court; Rain! Rain!; Please, Wind?; Snow Joe;* and *The New True Book of Holidays Around the World.*